THE WHOLE WORLD IS GOING CRAZY–BUT YOU DON'T HAVE TO

Scriptural *and* Psychological Healing

D1292391

JOE SIKORRA

The Whole WORLD is going CRAZY

BUT YOU DON'T HAVE TO

SCRIPTURAL AND
PSYCHOLOGICAL HEALING

Cover design and illustartions by
Enrique J. Aguilar

ISBN: 9798378598205

Unless otherwise stated, all Sacred Scripture quotes are taken from NABRE
(New American Bible Revised Edition)

WHAT PEOPLE ARE SAYING

"With all the passion, clarity, and humor you enjoyed for years on the radio, Joe now offers his insights in this book. Solutions for your problems, based on the best of psychology and scripture. Work these words into your life!"

—**Drew Mariani**, Relevant Radio host

"Science and faith are paths to a loving life. *The Whole World is Going Crazy—But You Don't Have To* is a brilliant weaving of the best scientific findings and spiritual principles for leading a fulfilling life. Joe Sikorra has provided excellent tools for creating and sustaining excellence and enthusism in times of adversity."

—**Robert Maurer, Ph.D.** Clinical Psychologist Faculty, UCLA School of Medicine

"I write words on a blank piece of paper, then I work with actors and directors to create a show we hope you'll enjoy. But this is your life. Joe's inspiring book will help you create the life—your life—that you want to see"

—**Ed Solomon**, writer of *Men in Black*, the *Bill & Ted* movies

"As a film score composer, I write music to help breathe life into movies. This book will help breathe life into your soul!"

—**John Debney**, composer of *The Passion of the Christ*

"In a world that can sometimes feel out of control and filled with challenges, Joe Sikorra's book is a bright light. In a conversational way that draws the reader in, Joe lets us know that it IS possible for us to make small changes every day and to live with purpose, meaning and great joy. As he weaves psychology and faith together, Joe offers a roadmap for how to "Become what you believe." While it is well suited for all of us, it has a particularly inspiring and comforting message for young adults who are struggling to find hope in the world around them. If you are looking for a book that will be a companion to you on your journey to a more inspired, more meaningful, more joyful life, this *is* that book. It will fill you with the hope and joy you are seeking and will inspire you to encourage others around you to do the same."

—**Shannon M. Clancy,** Chief Executive Officer, The Rob and Melani Walton Endowed CEO

"Joe is a carpenter of the soul, and here he shares a full toolbox inspired by his deep faith and personal experience, offering practical, proven tools to help repair or build a better life."

—**Michael Bostick,** Producer, Emmy award-winning television producer and veteran film executive

"Trying to summarize the variety of wise insights and prudent advice in this new book by Joe Sikorra is like trying to describe the variety of foods that await you in a large, well-stocked supermarket. From sound guidance on marriage issues, dealing with past hurts, relationship difficulties, and how to truly know yourself, to how you can find true happiness and joy in your life, it's all here. There's so much good packed into these pages, you'll just have to read it for yourself. Enjoy!"

—**Patrick Madrid,** Catholic Apologist, Author: *Surprised by Truth, The Godless Delusion: A Catholic Challenge to Modern Atheism* and *A Year with the Bible.*

"This is a powerful book at a critical time for our culture and our world. With mental health issues on the rise, together with falling rates of belief in God and the practice of religion, Joe's discussion of contemporary mental health issues speaks to the heart of the matter for all of us. Combining psychology, science, and the Christian faith, this book has something in it for everyone. As a practicing healthcare provider, I find that his wisdom and guidance are spot on. As a practicing Catholic Christian, his weaving of Scripture and sound faithful advice into every section gave his analysis extra power. This book was extremely helpful to me, too! I highly recommend Joe's book to anyone wanting to gain insight and assistance with the psychological and spiritual struggles of our time."

—**Christopher Tolcher**, M.D., F.A.A.P

"As a long-time married gal, the chapters on marriage spoke to me. I look forward to all of my kids "choosing wisely," but I especially look forward to giving a copy to my son and his new wife as well as to my daughter and future son-in-law as they begin their respective marriages and parenting journey. My hope is that they all "see what is best in each other" as so eloquently stated by Joe."

—**Kelly Griffin**, Wife, Mom, Grandma, and a Texan to the bone!

"… with sixty years of pastoral ministry behind me—I am impressed with [this] work. Straight-forward, solid, functional, rational, biblical counsel. I especially like the "Next Steps" suggestions. All of us whom counsel know that we must seek to bridge the disconnect between the counselee feeling good following a session, believing they can move on toward a positive solution but who are given little specific counsel about the individual steps which make up the journey out of the dilemma. Your work is broad-based and will be therapeutic to a wide range of specific mental/moral dilemmas. I highly commend it. You are, indeed, a writer, Joe!"

—**Bill Anderson**, long-time Baptist pastor

"Joe Sikorra is a gifted therapist and writer, but it is his own life's journey through crisis that has given him a special ability to communicate with anyone who may be despairing in what can seem, like a very crazy world indeed! Joe fills each page, with practical insights and actionable steps, to help people navigate many of life's most challenging issues. This book is an invaluable tool to help anyone work towards a modern, creative and positive approach to mental and spiritual fitness!"

—**Clint Carmichael**, Actor / Producer

"Joe Sikorra's newest book, *The Whole World is Going Crazy—But You Don't Have To* shows us how to take simple tasks and infuse them with meaning and purpose to understand how to live with the grace that God offers each of us. This moving account explores not only how to love others but to love ourselves—to run, to fall, to get back up, and ultimately to run to win in a world that so desperately needs this important and inspiring message."

—**Steve Zabilski**, Executive Director, Saint Vincent de Paul, Phoenix

"I looked forward to reading Joe Sikorra's second book as I thoroughly enjoyed his first effort, *Defying Gravity*, which was as inspirational as it was heartwarming. I was not disappointed. His second book, *The World Is Going Crazy—But You Don't Have To*, is full of easy-to-comprehend wisdom and practical solutions to everyday issues, written in a way only a person with experience, expertise and passion can. It's a manual for solving life's problems in a practical and entertaining way. I'll be keeping this one on my nightstand permanently!"

—**Greg Fitzpatrick**, Hollywood Stuntman

"Few people can write with the clarity, wisdom, and humor of Joe Sikorra. His style is both engaging and practical! And as a personal friend, I know that he has walked the talk—he is a man of integrity and his words are trustworthy. I loved this book, and strongly encourage anyone interested in living a hope-filled life to pick it up today!"

—**Rev. Dr. Ross Porter**, Anglican Clergy, Founder of Stillpoint Family Resources

"Joe has written a how-to guide showing where faith intersects with psychology in a practical and applicable way… Reading this book, you will develop life skills such as faith filled perseverance and resilience to handle life's ups and downs."

—**Timmerie M.A.**, Host of Trending with Timmerie

Joe Sikorra manages to accomplish the one thing we need from a book like this, at a time like this … Concise, well thought out, practical, and most importantly "biblical" steps to achieve calm in the storm of our present-day events. You're actually able to finish the book and apply that which you read and see results immediately. That cup of cool water to all of us who need it. Thanks, Joe!

—**James Arnold Taylor**, Actor/Writer/Podcaster (Star Wars: The Clone Wars)

"The whole world is going crazy" … and so am I. We've all recently suffered through a two-year COVID-19 shutdown. Trapped inside our homes, working remotely, wearing masks and keeping socially-distanced like lepers took a tremendous toll on our relationships, on our careers and on our self-image and understanding.More than ever, our lives are fraught with depression, anxiety, frayed relationships and a suffocating sense of despair and helplessness. Joe Sikorra's new book, *The Whole World Is Going Crazy—But You Don't Have To* has come out at exactly the right time. More than ever, we all need the tools that Joe offers to heal ourselves, our relationships and our outlook on life, to get back on track and become the person God intended us to be. As a professional marriage and family therapist, Joe Sikorra challenges us to envision that person, to banish our fears and doubts and to get on with the business of living a happy, fulfilled and blessed life, a life of gratitude, purpose and meaning, a life worth living and sharing with those we love. Thank you, Joe, for this welcomed and insightful book!"

—**Dr. Bill Creasy**, UCLA Department of English, (ret.) Founder, Logos Bible Study

"I can't really think of a time when I read a book and felt like the author was there with me (and answered all my questions). This book feels more like an 8-hour live therapy session that you wish everyone you know had attended.It is no secret that the world is indeed going crazy; we are reminded of it every day. However, in this brilliant book, Joe shows us a path to complete sanity. As a true man of faith, he speaks in clear and concise easy-to-digest language, so that we can all understand—while reaching tremendous spiritual depth.
In what could only be rightly described as "Christo-therapy," the author conjures the perfect blend between pop psychology and Sacred Scripture, like a true winemaker. In these pages you will find healing and, in every chapter, the "next steps" to change and sustain those positive changes in your life—And the world will be a little less crazy. Keep this book close. Thank you, Joe Sikorra."

—**Marta Pinto**, Former School Principle and Teacher, La Floresta.

"I gave much physically, emotionally, and psychologically during my 27 years as a Police Officer ... serving people daily in their times of crisis and conflict. Their life experiences became my life experiences. Joe Sikorra and I were partners for many of those years on Patrol. We labored side by side to protect and serve our community. I trusted and relied upon him to have my back and to keep me safe, as he did me. Through his words in this book he continues to protect, serve, and partner with us all in navigating the stress and pressures of life."

—**Michael Graham**, Police Sergeant (Retired)

"As a baseball coach, teacher, and Dean of Students, It is my job to educate and shape character. And most of all, I try to do this by personal example. This book has inspired me to continue to look at my life so that I can help mentor those around me."

—Steve Sotir

DEDICATION

For my wife, Lori, I can't imagine facing the crazy without you; and my son, Benjamin, your laughter brings light into the darkness. I love you both deeply.

And...

For Bob Maurer, Ph.D., my mentor and dear friend, who provided the spark by saying, "Joe, I think you'd be an excellent therapist...." The spark has become a flame.

And finally ...

For my clients ... I hope I have been worthy of your trust.

CONTENTS

FOREWORD

by Fr. Dave Heney, Pastor

Joe Sikorra has led a remarkable life, filled with the highest highs and the lowest lows, and he shares the wisdom of both with you in this amazing book on living a normal and healthy life in a crazy world. This is a welcome book! Clear, concise, and compelling advice on coping with life today is needed now more than ever. After all, you are bombarded every day with all kinds of crazy social media claims, disturbing news events, perhaps your own fears and worries, or just the challenging events of everyday marriage and family life. No need to panic. The answers are here in very easy-to-understand ideas.

Joe writes as he talks. As you read this book you will begin to feel you are sitting in a comfortable chair across from a trusted friend and engaged in a fascinating conversation. Very few writers have this skill. Joe does.

I have known Joe for over 25 years both as a valued friend and, most important, as an amazingly insightful and effective therapist to the people I have sent to him from my parish. I always have the highest confidence in Joe to help the people I entrust to him. We also worked together for several years on Relevant Radio on the live call-in show "The Joe Sikorra Show with Fr. Dave." In that challenging two hours of live on-air broadcast, I always heard Joe offer just the right advice to callers desperately in need of wisdom and guidance.

Joe continues his work in his local therapy practice now, as well as reaching a wider audience as a podcaster with entertaining and helpful short episodes integrating faith and psychology. There is much wisdom in these episodes. I hope you will find them.

Finally, I am glad that the wisdom of Joe Sikorra is now available in this book format that will help far more people than can ever come to his office. Very good news for this crazy world!

INTRODUCTION

It used to be a cliché: The whole world is going crazy! Now it feels true.

Why has the world gone crazy? There isn't one reason, but probably a thousand, including: Covid, inflation, hyper partisan politics, war with other nations, war with our neighbors and family, and war within ourselves.

The bad news? You can't change the world. But you *can* change your own life for the better. How does it begin?

There are many excellent secular books written on the science of happiness and resilience. Countless books written by brilliant theologians speak about picking up your cross and following God. But in this book, I share the best of the psychological research and the faith necessary to achieve your best life—a life beyond mere sanity.

When Jesus called out to Peter, "Follow me," Peter did so by literally dropping what he knew—his fishing net—and walking away into something unknown. (Matt. 4:18-20) And so did the other disciples who were called. Letting go isn't always easy—even if it's your pain or dysfunction. Why? Because it's familiar. Familiar feels safe. But Peter would not have become the great leader in the church had he not let go.

God may be asking you to let go as well. Of what? Your anxiety, shame, addiction, need to control—the list goes on. Maybe you're ready, but you don't know how. You may not even know why you act this way, feel like you do, or believe as you do. You're not alone. The first step, however, may be to let go. But remember, you're letting go to follow God—and a better life.

I know the pain and joy of letting go all too well. Both of my boys were born with a terminal disease. Talk about beginnings and endings so intertwined. I had to let go of my dreams for my boys. I had to let go of my hopes, plans, and life as I knew it. I had to let go of life as I hoped it would be. "Let go, Joe," I heard God quietly whisper. "Trust."

Defying Gravity, my first book, is a personal memoir chronicling my family's journey. After its publication, I thought I was done. With writing books, I mean. It was the fulfillment of a dream and, I believe, a call. When speaking about my book, I'd frequently say, "I'm not really a writer, but …" False humility? Maybe. Then my publisher heard me say that once and reminded me they had published my book: "SO STOP SAYING YOU'RE NOT A WRITER!", they politely reminded me. Okay … I'm a writer.

Due to my personal life experience, and my chosen profession as a Marriage and Family Therapist, I am constantly thinking about what makes for the good life and how best to achieve it. I could have held on and tried to do things my way. But that would have been crazy. God had a better plan for me. And He has a better plan for you! Whereas *Defying Gravity* is about how God worked in my family's life, this book is how He can work in yours!

It took me only the umpteenth time for friends, family, and clients to say to me, "The whole world is going crazy!" And me responding, "But you don't have to," to know that this was the next book I wanted to write. Once I had the title, the book flowed.

It's a profound honor to help people move through their darkness and into the light. I am the objective outsider invited into peoples' lives in a very personal way. A deep bond is created between client and therapist. It is essential, however, that I remain objective to see where you are, help you to see where you are, help you understand how you've gotten there, and most importantly, the path toward healing.

You may not know why you feel anxious, react with anger, feel helpless, constantly feel that you're going to be abandoned, etc. But there are reasons. You may not know right now how to improve your marriage, become more resilient, or get free from addiction—but you can. I wrote this book to help you gain insight and provide a roadmap.

When clients share their struggles and burdens, and have come out the other side, I'd say their lives are better, richer, and filled with more purpose and meaning. Not despite the struggle—but because of the struggle. I wish you all the blessings life offers, but despite my fervent prayers and wishes, you will hit roadblocks and setbacks—and I submit, this is for your good! (More on this later.)

Having worked thousands of hours with people in crises, and many thousands more immersed in the study, I've identified many of the thought and behavioral patterns that cause distress. You wouldn't go to a therapist with the goal of only sharing your problems, however. You want—and deserve—solutions based on science, research, and Scripture. That's right. You don't have to drop your faith when looking for answers to your psychological problems—just the opposite. God has given you all the tools you need to experience transformation and growth. The more I've learned, the more I've come to recognize that the best of psychology is also consistent with Scripture and the Christian walk.

You've been given this incredible gift: life. It is precious. It is fleeting. Are you living your best life, or do you feel you may be following the crazy train?

It's incredible that the same God who said, Pick up your cross and follow me, also gives you the capacity to heal from the wounds as you follow, as well as from the scars that have been inflicted on you or you've inflicted on yourself. Just as your body can heal from an injury, your brain and psyche can heal if you take the proper steps.

This book includes many of the themes and problems I encounter in my chosen profession: trauma, anxiety, depression, focus, abuse, meaning and purpose, forgiveness versus reconciliation, social media, and more. I address these problems—and, more importantly, the solutions—as a clinician and a lover of my faith.

Some chapters may resonate with you more than others. But if you read a chapter and say to yourself, yeah, I already got this, it may give you some insight into how and why someone close to you acts and believes as they do. Equipped with that knowledge, you can become that compassionate friend, spouse, or neighbor to journey with others as you move toward a saner life.

I purposely wrote this to be a concise book. When I came up with the title, "The Whole World is Going Crazy—But You Don't Have To," I wrote with particular urgency. So many people are struggling. You may be among them. So I undertook this work as though the house were on fire. Run in. Rescue the people and the animals, grab a few valuables and start dousing the place with water.

At first glance, you may look at the various chapters and correctly note that I cover many topics. How can one book cover so many different themes and still have merit? The truth is each chapter could be an entire book. Actually, there are hundreds of books each on each chapter. I have read many of these books and have worked to give you the big takeaways. But my goal in this work is to not be exhaustive in depth with each topic. Instead, I want to open the door so that you can look in and say, "Oh yeah. That makes sense," and then be able to grab the tools you need so you can move from the crazy to a more sane life. I firmly believe that if you take in what is written, then follow it up with action steps, you will discover a life that is not just saner, but a life that is vibrant and joyful.

Each chapter has three essential elements. The first part is to help you to define the problem. You can't fix what you don't understand. For instance, in the guilt and shame chapters, I illuminate their differences. Why and how is guilt good, and why and how is shame destructive? You may be conflating the two, and you may not fully understand which one it is you feel. Without that clarity, you may never escape the clutches and pain of both. I then dive deeper into the roots. Why do you feel shame? What are its origins, and how is it affecting you and your relationships now? I offer insights based on psychological research, anecdotal evidence, and Scripture.

The second element is the path forward. How do you recover, grow, and get beyond the shame and guilt? Again, this is all supported by the research and Scripture.

The third element is the reflection questions at the end of each chapter. I call this "Next Steps." These are questions for reflection as well as exercises or action steps. It's easy to spend just a few minutes on these or even skip them entirely, but seriously, take your time with the exercises. I suggest you reflect and work on them with another person or small group. Together, you may find more inspired ways to make a change toward a saner, better, and more joyful life.

After reading and reflecting on what I wrote, I hope you become inspired to dive even deeper into your life, your faith, and what you believe. I want you to think of me as your companion as you figure out what you need to do to escape the insanity and live a rich, whole, and purposeful life.

God says, "Be doers of the word and not hearers only" (James 1:22,). In other words, knowing Scripture and what makes for a good and holy life is not enough. You have to live it out. So, too, the information in this book can give you insight into living a better, more godly life—but you have to take the steps if you want to heal and avoid the insanity.

Your life isn't just about what you've been given. It is about *what you do* with what you've been given. Whatever your life is now, it can be more. That's God's call.

It does seem that the whole world is going crazy. But you don't have to. You can choose where to go from here. Let's see how—together.

1

BECOME WHAT YOU BELIEVE
(PART 1)

I LOVE SCRIPTURE. I SOMETIMES FIND THE QUESTIONS JESUS asks more interesting than what He says. Again, sometimes. The Gospel of Matthew, chapter 9, is one of those times.

Two blind men are following Jesus. No easy task, I'm sure. They are blind, after all. He was toward the end of another ordinary extraordinary day: healing a woman who had been hemorrhaging for years, followed by raising a little girl from the dead. The blind men kept calling out to Jesus. "Mercy, Lord! Mercy!" He kept walking toward His house.

Did He hear them? Probably. Was He spent and too tired to help another person out? I doubt that—Jesus had stamina. He'd preach for days and then put on a meal for thousands. (More on that later.)

When Jesus got home, they followed Him in. And then comes the question: "Do you really believe I can do this?" He asked.

This question haunts me. It does not make me scared, but it gives me great pause—and it should for you too! What if they hemmed and hawed and said, "Well ... maybe? Um, not sure ... Can you?" The question, luckily, didn't hang in the air for long. They immediately responded, "Yes!" Their belief was unwavering. Fully committed. And what happened? Jesus said, "Become what you believe," and they were healed right then and there!

Some success gurus and other motivational speakers promote the idea, "You can achieve anything if you just believe!" Simply, that's a lie. No scientific evidence supports this, and it certainly is not biblically supported. Yes, as I've just said, belief matters—a lot! But I can believe all I want that I am 6'2", 250 pounds, and play running back for the Los Angeles Rams, still it will not make it so. I'll just have to be satisfied with my not-so-massive 5'10", 175 pounds.

All miracles reported in Scripture were of God working through the faithful who believed that *He, God,* could accomplish the seemingly impossible. And to me, this is excellent news! Your faith *in you* will vacillate and sometimes (if not frequently) falter. What you believe about yourself and what you can achieve can change moment by moment.

If you have a great day and everything breaks your way, you'll be more inclined to believe in a brighter future. Conversely, if you get bad news or are tired or hungry or stuck in traffic or ... it will affect your mood, which can, in turn, affect what you believe about yourself and your future. But remember what Jesus asked the blind men, "Do you believe *I* can do this?" Not, do you believe you can make this happen? No particular mantra or positive thoughts would bring about their healing. Instead, it was their believing prayer and their faith in God that allowed the miraculous to occur.

Another great question/healing time was when Jesus met a man at a pool called Bethesda. This story is told in the Gospel of John, chapter 5. The man had been an invalid for thirty-eight years. Some thought the pool had healing powers. Many blind and lame people would gather near the pool, and when the waters were stirred up, they'd race in, hoping to be healed (again, not an easy task if you're an invalid). The first one in had the best shot.

The man was persistent. He'd been at it for years, but his faith was misplaced. He believed *in the water.* He was going to the wrong place for healing. But he was about to meet the Author and Healer of all creation, Jesus Christ. But again, before any healing, Jesus asked him, "Do you even want to be healed?" It's a fascinating question. It wasn't rhetorical. You'd assume that the answer would be an obvious yes. But not so quick ...

Ask yourself, do I want to be healed? You'd probably answer immediately with, "Yes! Of course (you idiot)!" And how did the man at the pool answer? He began with a bunch of excuses.

"You see, when the waters get stirred up, everyone who can walk is faster, has the right help, etc...." or something like that. He didn't answer Jesus's question. He just offered excuses. I'm not saying they were lame excuses. (No pun intended.) He was right. He had it rough. But that wasn't what Jesus asked. He didn't ask him why he wasn't healed. He asked if he *wanted* to be healed.

Now ask yourself again. Do I want to be healed? If you, too, come up with many wonderful excuses, you might be kidding yourself.

How often have you looked at other people and asked, "Why don't they just … (fill in the blank)?" Their life would be so much better. As the Good Book says, it's easy to see the sliver in another person's eye and miss the plank in your own. Do you want to be healed?

In the world of psychology, this is sometimes called secondary gains. You might be accountable for living your life differently if you are healed. You might have to get a job. Go back to school. Be kind to your spouse. Admit that you were wrong. (God forbid.)

With healing comes responsibility. If you continue to lie on the ground, you won't have to finish the race. And again, running is hard. But you've been admonished: run to win!

When the lame man was done offering excuses, Jesus didn't raise his face to heaven and begin a long prayer. He simply commanded the man to get up, grab his bedroll, and start walking. And he did! He was called to act—and so will you if you want to be healed and live the resilient, resurrection life God offers.

Again, the two questions Jesus asked these men are questions you must first ask yourself. What do *you* believe about the capacity for your life to change, to be healed? Remember, it's not *if you think you* can create a miracle. Do you believe *God can heal you*? And if your life does change, are you ready to act differently?

Back when I was in the police academy, the instructors illustrated the power of belief and its life-and-death consequences. They showed us video clips of shootings where officers were shot—not the most compelling recruiting video. But we had already signed on the dotted line. Though inflicted with what should have been a mortal wound, one officer lived. Another, though the wounds were not life-threatening, died. Why? Belief. The officer who survived simply refused to give up his life. I don't know what kind of religious beliefs the officer had. But he refused to give up. He believed he could live. Remember the man at the Pool of Bethesda? He believed that healing was possible—for thirty-eight years!

And so began that particular aspect of our police training. Survival isn't just about belief, absent sweat, and persistence. That specific training culminated in a day aptly named the Will to Survive. They worked us out beyond exhaustion, then put us in the ring and had us duke it out, wearing sufficient padding to prevent real damage. It was brutal. You had to rise above what you thought your body could do and push on to survival. It took grit. Determination. And belief.

I could speak of numerous stories of people who have achieved unbelievable things because of faith, belief, and will. Not just the great saints who performed miracles, sometimes even subjecting themselves to torture and sacrificing their lives, but sports teams who overcame huge obstacles to achieve victory; authors who—despite tremendous rejection and hardship—became billion-dollar writers like J.K Rowling, the author of the Harry Potter series.

Before finally being published, Rowling was turned down by twelve different publishers. And before she even began to write the books, she had spent five years planning the series, mapping it out in great detail. I don't know what role faith played in sustaining Rowling through the years of writing and rejection. What I do believe, however, is that if she did not have great belief and faith in her work, she would never have succeeded.

Faith isn't the absence of all doubt. There will be times when you step back from your quest and question. But faith and belief—particularly if you feel called by God to pursue your goal—will give you strength to endure, even when a part of you feels too weak to go on in the face of opposition and setbacks.

Although numerous decisions affect how our lives will turn out regarding health outcomes, like genetics, eating right, and exercise, belief also factors in considerably. In one study, middle-aged adults with more positive beliefs about aging lived an average of 7.6 years longer than those with more negative beliefs, even when controlling for current health and other risk factors.[1] Additionally, optimistic people were less likely to develop heart disease, again controlling for other risk factors. [2]

Belief is an acceptance of a claim likely to be true. Optimism is slightly different and could be understood as a tendency to expect the best possible outcome. Matthew 7:11 speaks about God's desire to give you good gifts. Of course, not everything we ask of God in prayer is given to us if it isn't going to be good for us. But when you wholeheartedly seek God's will and fight to achieve the good and right, you have a strong ally in God.

But again, belief alone is not like having a magic wand. You can't decide to eat bags of chips and a half-pound of bacon every night for dinner and expect a good health outcome. (Mmmm. Now I'm hungry.) But your positive belief will foster the desire to make healthy choices. Faith leads to action.

To live a resilient, faith-filled life, you have to believe, but you must also act. You must cooperate with God. He doesn't just push you around and make you what He wants you to be. He isn't a tyrant. Consider how you might have to act, working with God's grace, if you want your life to change. Here are a few examples:

Peter was fishing with his companions (Luke 5). They had been at it all night. I hate shift work, but a guy's gotta do what a guy's gotta do. They caught squat. This is not to be confused with squid. But *nada*— my usual fishing experience. In the morning, they were cleaning their nets. Jesus told them to go back out and cast again. (Ugh.) "Master," they said, "we've been at this all night," and blah, blah, blah. "But if

[1] Levy BR, Slade MD, Kunkel SR, Kasl SV. Longevity increased by positive self-perceptions of aging. J Pers Soc Psychol. 2002 Aug;83(2):261-70. doi: 10.1037//0022-3514.83.2.261. PMID: 12150226.

[2] Rozanski A, Bavishi C, Kubzansky LD, Cohen R. Association of Optimism With Cardiovascular Events and All-Cause Mortality: A Systematic Review and Meta-analysis. JAMA Netw Open. 2019 Sep 4;2(9):e1912200. doi: 10.1001/jamanetworkopen.2019.12200. PMID: 31560385; PMCID: PMC6777240.

you say so ..." They made the extra effort and hit the mother lode. They filled their boats with fish! It was a miraculous catch. Their boats nearly sank because of the number of fish. Imagine their joy! Think World's Deadliest Catch without the crabs. Note He didn't do this for them at the beginning of their shift. They had already worked hard. They were exhausted. Now ask yourself, when do you give up? What causes you to stop believing?

Another great story ... Jesus was with his disciples while He preached, taught, and healed—for three days. Maybe we should be more patient when our pastors or priests get long-winded. I've never heard a three-day sermon. Think about how tired He must have been. But Jesus wasn't done. He looked at the people and saw that they were hungry. Then He asked his disciples how much bread they had. They had a few loaves of bread and a couple of fish. It was not enough to feed the thousands present. But He didn't just say, no sweat, I got this. He asked them to give him the little they had. It wasn't a lot. But it was also *all* they had. He took it, multiplied it, and fed them all—with leftovers to boot!

We are not gods. We can't just will things into existence with positive thoughts. But God does offer us His grace. And when you couple that with your belief, which leads you to act and engage in the struggle, the miraculous is possible. I've seen marriages on the brink of divorce transform into loving unions; I've witnessed people rise out of despair and depression and overcome the debilitation of anxiety; I've seen grief give way to joy. I could go on and on about how people have transformed their lives. But I've yet to see anyone do any of these things without changing their belief about what is possible (faith) and then taking action. As the apostle James says, "Indeed someone may say, 'You have faith and I have works.' Demonstrate your faith to me without works, and I will demonstrate my faith to you from my works" (James 2:18). Faith and works, works and faith—they fit together.

You might look at your own life and recognize the obvious: you don't have enough to accomplish what God wants you to do or what you want to do. Just like the disciples, you may think you're inadequately provisioned. And yet He might still ask everything of you. But He can take the little you have and accomplish the miraculous! You must ask yourself if you are willing to give what little you have to God. Become what you believe.

Next Steps ...

- What are you holding on to that God might ask you to let go of? Addiction? Fear? Anger? Your plans?

- If you trusted God to help you make a change in your life, knowing that you couldn't do it on your own, what change would you make?

- What examples do you have from your own life experience when things had worked out, even when you were sure they wouldn't or didn't know how they would?

- Is your belief based on what you think you can accomplish or what God can achieve in your life?

- What things or people cause your belief to falter? Are there things you can do or people you can include in your life that can help support and foster your belief?

2

BECOME WHAT YOU BELIEVE
(PART II)

I F I ASKED YOU WHO YOU ARE, WHAT WOULD YOU SAY?
You may begin to list roles you play as a mother or father; you might tell me your occupation or religious orientation, educational background, marital status, etc. And if we were at a cocktail party and you weren't interested in talking to me (which sometimes happens), those brief descriptions might suffice. Small talk. Done. Off to get another cocktail.

But let's say you found this question interesting, and we began a lengthy conversation. Eventually, we'd move beyond roles you play, physical attributes, etc., and plumb the depths of how you see the world and yourself. And being the socially curious guy I am, I might continue asking you when you began to believe this or that about yourself. Was it in your early twenties when your brain was fully developed? Was it as a teen that you "discovered" yourself? Or earlier, like when your diaper was changed (or not)? At this point, you might think that one of us has had too many cocktails, and perhaps you misheard me, or I was no longer making sense. But being polite, you don't pretend to make eye contact with someone across the room and excuse yourself. Instead, you ask, "Diapers? What do you mean, Joe?"

You see, we are unbelievable information-processing machines. From birth until the day we die, we continually take in information about the world, then pass judgment on it, and take in information about ourselves, usually based on how others see and treat us—and that's when it gets tricky …

One day, Jesus conversed with his disciples, and He asked them what people were saying about the Son of Man. Jesus was referring to Himself. (Matt. 16).

They said some think He is John the Baptizer, some say, Elijah, some Jeremiah, or one of the other prophets. They didn't know who Jesus was. Then Jesus asked Peter directly. Who do you think I am, Peter?

"The Messiah," Peter said.

Bull's-eye!

But then the critical statement, in my opinion, came next.

"And now," Jesus said, "I am going to tell you who you are, Peter!"

"You are a rock." Peter was the foundation upon which He was going to build His Church!

Impressive. No?

Now, why do I bring this up? Back to our cocktail conversation ...

As I said, you began taking in information about who you are from infancy. You may not consciously understand this, but when your diaper wasn't changed ; you weren't comforted during a thunderstorm; your caretaker constantly forgot to pick you up from school after practice; it was communicated that your wants and needs didn't matter; your boyfriend dumped you with no explanation; kids laughed at your uncool shoes (I still remember that one) or ... The list is endless, and of course, I'm sure it wasn't all negative, though that might be all you remember.

Hopefully, you experienced kind words and actions, loving touch, and encouragement. For most of us, it was a mixed bag. But your mind, consciously or unconsciously, interprets all these words, actions, and events, and you form a belief about who you are.

For you to experience resilience and to live the life that God says you can live, you must allow your belief about *whom you think you are* to be reshaped by God.

Scripture doesn't say how Peter responded to Jesus's assertion that he was a rock, but I suspect he initially had a hard time taking it in. After all, when Jesus performed the miraculous catch of fish I referred to earlier, Peter's response was to ask Jesus to leave him because Peter saw himself as unworthy. Peter's response was based on shame—Jesus saw him differently.

Every opportunity you encounter, every relationship you experience, your mood, and even the chances you take will be shaped by how you see yourself.

Allow me to elaborate by playing a little psychological game. I'm going to ask you only one question. And just to prepare you, when I ask this question to a large audience, I'd say that roughly 99% of people answer incorrectly. Now, I don't relish proving you wrong, but I want to help you change your mind about a fundamental concept of belief. Ready?

Question: Is rejection painful, yes or no?

Now, if you're honest (and like the 99%), you'll probably scan your memory and think about the time you didn't get the job, your girlfriend dumped you, didn't get picked for the team (or go ahead and think about your own rejection experience).

Should you take the money and go home? Indeed, the answer seems obvious. Rejection *is* painful. Right?

You go for it. "Rejection is painful, Joe."

"Final answer?"

You hesitate a moment…. "Final answer."

"Wrong," I say.

[Insert tires screeching, bombs going off, the sound of drinks being spilled, and a general cacophony of murmur, murmur, murmur.]

Before you close this book and pitch it into the fireplace, let me illustrate why you think rejection is painful with a simple story but with two different endings….

Take one:

Your best friend sets you up on a blind date. You're super excited.

"It's been a while," you say to yourself.

You put together your best outfit. One that says, "I'm casual," but also enough to say, "I care." (I have no idea what that would be—fashion not being my strongest suit.)

You remind yourself to be polite and curious. You get a reservation at that oh-so-difficult restaurant to get into. The night is superb, you tell yourself. You think that this really could go somewhere. You hope.

Then, at the end of the night, you muster up the courage necessary and ask your date if you could have another one next weekend. She turns to you with those beautiful green eyes that you've already fallen in love with, and she says, "I don't think so. I have to wash my dog."

A beat, then: "All weekend?"

"Pretty much," she says. "And I'll probably be a little too busy for the rest of my life. Sorry."

You stare blankly at the outside of her door that she just slammed. And after you manage to close your mouth and let the shock slowly wear off your face, you say, "I'm such an idiot! Of course, she doesn't want to go out with me again. I'm a loser! Just more proof that I'll never find love! Hopefully, I can go home and pray my cat doesn't feign indifference." (Good luck.)

Okay. I agree. That's pretty painful. But before you think I've just solidified your belief that rejection is painful, let's try again.

Take two:

Your best friend sets you up on a blind date. You're super excited.

"It's been a while," you say to yourself.

You put together your best outfit. One that says, "I'm casual," but also enough to say, "I care."

You remind yourself to be polite and curious. You get a reservation at that oh-so-difficult restaurant to get into. The night is superb, you tell yourself. You think that this really could go somewhere. You hope.

Then, at the end of the night, you muster up the courage necessary and ask your date if you could have another one next weekend. She turns to you with those beautiful green eyes that you've already fallen in love with, and she says, "I don't think so. I have to wash my dog."

"All weekend?" you ask.

"Pretty much," she says. "And I'll probably be a little too busy for the rest of my life. Sorry."

Now I'm going to let you think about your answer for a minute before I ask you again, "Is rejection painful?"

With even greater vehemence, you and everyone around you shouts, "Yes, Joe. Rejection is painful!"

But wait! This time, instead of the harsh tongue lashing you gave yourself in take one, you speak differently to yourself: In an alternate ending, you say to yourself, "You know what? This was one date. Relationships are meant to be cultivated, and this is something I can do. I'm a good person. I'm kind, loving, and generous. I've done much work making the most of my life. There's a good chance that someone will find my traits desirable. Let this one go. I might have saved myself from continuing a relationship with the wrong person! God sees a larger context."

Now I ask you. Is rejection painful, or is it what you believe about yourself?

Mic drop.

I'm not suggesting that this is easy. Particularly if you've experienced significant rejection early on, but just like learning new skills, you can learn to speak to yourself differently. You can see yourself differently. How? It begins by allowing yourself to be loved by God. To let Him tell you who you are.

"You are a rock, Peter," Jesus said.

Peter needed to see himself differently—through the eyes of Love incarnate.

You, too, need to see yourself differently. You are God's most precious creation. As Psalm 139 says, God formed you in your mother's womb. You are a wonderful creation.

No matter what you've done, as is told in the story of the Prodigal Son (Luke 15), God is ready to take you back. He wants to wrap you up in His arms and celebrate. We will reflect more on this important story on the chapters about guilt and shame, particularly from the point of view of guilt and shame—and the difference between the two. In later chapters, I will also explore how your early childhood experiences have shaped your negative, self-rejecting thoughts and beliefs and how they are triggered in your current life. And most importantly, how with faith and work, you can reshape those negative beliefs into ones that are more functional and life-affirming.

For too long, you've lived a life defined by how others have treated and defined you. God says that you are worthy. He has chosen to dwell within you. He is moving you and guiding you and reshaping you. It's time to let God tell you who you are. He created you to live with Him for all eternity. He has chosen to place His Spirit inside you. If the God of all creation lives within you, then indeed, you can live differently, joyfully, with resilience, purpose, and meaning. Become what you believe.

Next Steps ...

- Whom have you allowed to define you?

- How would you rather see yourself?

- How would you live differently if you believed you were indeed a son or daughter of God, and He takes a personal interest in your life?

- How do you respond when you feel rejected?

- How do you speak about yourself and reject yourself?

- What words would you use to speak to a friend who needed encouragement? What tone would you use? Could you now use this model and apply it to yourself?

3

CHANGE

AS A THERAPIST, I CONSIDER MYSELF TO BE IN THE *changing* business. I enjoy home makeover shows because it's fun to watch the physical transformation of a structure—the change. But my favorite programs or stories are about human transformation—far more complex an endeavor. How *do you* change? But perhaps the better question you should ask is how do you make and *sustain* the positive change you want to make?

I will get to the *how* to make change momentarily. But first, you might want to ask yourself if there are things in your life that you ought to change. How do you know if a change is essential for you right now? What are the signs? Your body and brain will give you clues. What are they?

If you feel that your life lacks meaning, make a change. If you're stressed out, it's an excellent time to make a change. If you find yourself with a longer list of regrets than accomplishments; if you're lacking joy; if your marriage is in crisis; if you're engaging in self-destructive habits; if you've lost interest in life; if you're more about the excuses and not acting; if you feel trapped—if any of these clues resonate, don't get depressed—make a change. You can do it!

God calls you to a lifetime of growth and change. He wants your life to be transformed—and maybe you want that as well. I'm not talking about a new wardrobe that quickly becomes old or shedding a few pounds you put back on six months later. But creating habits that last and achieving goals will make you feel good about yourself.

What does God say about how much change He wants you to experience? Don't get discouraged, but He says He wants you to take on an entirely new way of life. A God-fashioned life. A life renewed from the inside out. (See Ephesians 4:22-24.) But how do you do that?

Let's break it down with a straightforward example that maybe you've experienced....

You want to get in better shape or lose weight. So January 1st rolls around, you join the gym, order all the miracle weight-loss food, and you're off to a great start! The pounds start coming off. You begin to see some muscle definition. Cool! But then a couple of months down the road and ...

Or let's say you want to grow in holiness, and step number one, you tell yourself, is to read the whole Bible. Nice goal! But then you get a few books in, and this person begets this person, and the numerous laws feel a little tedious, so you decide you don't need to read *the whole Bible*. Instead, you'll just jump to the Book of Matthew in the New Testament. I'm certainly not suggesting that Scripture is tedious—the entire Bible is worth reading and studying. What I am suggesting is that how you go about reading it matters, and in this case, it didn't work.

But go ahead and name your goal. Did you reach it? *Did you sustain the goal once you got there?* Whether you want to grow in holiness, lose weight, write a book, or do anything else you can imagine, you must think strategically.

If you want the best book, in my opinion, on strategy for making and sustaining change, I suggest you read my friend Robert Maurer's book, *Kaizen : How One Small Step Can Change Your Life*. But if you're too deeply engrossed in this book and can't even consider another book right now, I suggest you continue reading this chapter.

I want to begin with a personal example. I set the lofty goal of writing this book—and evidence that I made my goal is that you are reading it right now. But it was the strategy that enabled me to accomplish this goal.

A lofty goal begins with a dream. But dreams don't necessarily equate to action that leads to completion. Why? Fear.

What is the most difficult part if you think about some of your own lofty goals—and it's terrific to have them? For most of us, it's taking that first step.

If you attended school and were tasked with writing a significant paper, did you rush home and begin writing? Probably not. You may not have said you were "afraid" to write—but you may have procrastinated. Why? It seemed overwhelming—and the brain doesn't like overwhelming. Yet, if you address the brain's fear response, it will cooperate. You may be able to write a significant essay, but you must first address the fear factor.

Beginnings are scary. And the bigger the goal, the more frightening it is.

I've frequently told myself that I can't write a book. That isn't true. But the fear told me it was. "But," I tell myself, "I can write a sentence. And maybe a paragraph. And if I give myself some time, a page. Then a chapter …" You get the idea. The thought of writing a book is scary. But breaking it down into small, manageable steps allows you to begin; if only you first address the fear. You have far more capacity to accomplish goals and make change than you realize. And again, how do you do that? You break the goal into smaller steps until you say, "Yes. I can take that step." Then you begin to put those little steps together until you're beyond the fear. You've started. That's a huge hurdle. But only the first one. What's next?

Marathon runners talk about hitting the wall. It's those final few miles when they're just not sure they can finish. They've overcome the fear of the start, but finishing is another stumbling block. Again, to address "the wall," many runners take the same approach I'm suggesting you take when you start. You might not believe you can run another mile, much less five or so, but can you take one more step? Can you do a few more yards? It is one step after another until you cross that line.

I have dreamed of writing this book for a long time. But I didn't start until I sat with my mentor one day. I had the title but not much else—or so I thought. We brainstormed and came up with seven or so chapter ideas. Bam! That was it. I started writing that day. I knew the goal was to write a complete book, but the fear of writing a whole book prevented me from starting. I addressed the fear with a few lines written on my phone. Fear dissipated. Creativity opened up. That was the *strategy*. One sentence at a time. Yes. I also needed that human connection for the spark, to quiet the fear. But I just needed a couple of lines and a little encouragement, and then just the willingness to write a few more sentences at a time. That's what kept the fear meter turned off. Each time I sat in front of my computer with the blank screen, I didn't sit down to write a book—I sat down to write a sentence.

The truth is that I didn't write on any of the topics I had brainstormed with my friend. (Sorry, Bob.) But having those ideas out in front of me gave me the confidence to take the first small step.

I also permitted myself to write badly. Because honestly, the only bad words were the words that never saw the paper. Writing is the process of rewriting. Most of the words I initially wrote, I rewrote twice or ten times.

You have to allow yourself to fail. To write badly. Failure is the step you choose *not* to take. Fail. Fall. But then get back up. Take another step toward your goal and the change you want to make.

Believe it or not, this is also a biblical principle. What did Jesus say to his disciples when he first sent them out to preach the gospel? Start small. Don't begin by going to distant countries. Go to the houses right around you. Give someone a cup of water. That makes you a true apprentice. Give them the message. If they don't take it, wipe the dust from your Nike shoes and go on. (See Matthew chapter 10.) The disciples didn't "fail" because someone rejected the message. They were told to keep going—one step at a time. They did change the world. They did change their lives. But they did it one step and one house at a time.

Scripture speaks a great deal about fear and its negative consequences. Yet God also calls you to a life of growth and change. And probably the biggest impediment to change is fear. So, to make and sustain change, you must address fear! You can trust God to help you manage your fear, but that doesn't mean you are absolved from taking steps.

To make a change, you also need allies. I sat down with my friend Bob to address the fear, although I didn't admit that consciously. But think of this: God tells you that *He* is beside you and will not leave you as you grow and change as He has asked you. (See Deuteronomy 31:8.) Do not be discouraged, God says.

Whether you are trying to take your first small step or at mile 25 of your life's marathon, and you find yourself discouraged, afraid, or weary, remembering that you are not alone will give you a boost.

It's normal to experience fear and say, "I just don't have what it takes to make this change." That likely is fear talking—and fear can be pretty convincing. Some life coaches say that to overcome fear, you just have to believe in yourself. That might sound great as a mantra or on the front of a t-shirt, but it doesn't address the brain's fear response.

Psalm 18:2 reminds you that God is the rock! Not you. You might look at yourself and see that the task is too big. You're right. So, break it down into smaller steps until you can take that first small step.

You want to reach and sustain your goal, not just take a few small steps. But science says that creating practices and habits through small incremental steps will also more likely lead to habits that you sustain! To stay with our running example (and think of this as a metaphor for the change you want to make), if your goal was to run a marathon next year, the last thing in the world that you want to do is to hit the road and try to run it now. Not only will your body resist you, but your brain will also resist. Instead, if you go just a few yards farther each day, the change will be more easily adaptable and sustainable by your brain and body.

If you want to change your eating habits, you can apply this same principle. Let's say you love your burger and fries but know you must change that habit. Each time you sit down to eat, throw one French fry out before you begin your meal. Then the next time, two. That might sound funny, but you're addressing the essential aspect of making a change: fear. It's not as big a deal to toss out one of the fries, but the whole bunch? During your fry-disposing venture, you will probably conclude that you don't need the fries—because you gently created a new habit of eating less. Although it can work differently, it's not about making a big decision that leads to real change. It's about consistent, small steps.

Salespeople in the media understand and capitalize on this principle. Think about the television commercials you see. And see. And see [ad nauseam]. It's not the one spectacular commercial that gets you to buy their product. After the umpteenth time, you say, huh, I do need that new truck, soap, or whatever. It's repetition. Habit. That's why it's crucial that you must repeat what you can if you want to create and sustain change. Keep it doable.

Of course, asking what you want is the best way to begin making change. Are you willing to sacrifice to make a change? Do you know the new direction you want your life to take? It's OK not to have all the answers. As the great thinker, Voltaire said, "Don't let the perfect be the enemy of the good." You never will change if you feel you must be perfect. Don't set impossible standards for yourself. Expect setbacks.

One of the most significant predictors of making and sustaining change is what you say to yourself when you experience slips. You have a goal. Awesome. You begin taking those first few steps. Terrific! BUT … you must expect setbacks. Prepare yourself for this. To get back up and move toward your goal, you need to rehearse what you will say to yourself to provide you the strength to get back up and move forward again. For example, if your goal is to lose weight and you slip up and have a slice of pizza, don't get angry at yourself and say, "Well, I blew it! I might as well finish the whole pie." As you pursue change and experience setbacks, acknowledge that whatever you do may not be perfect—but then let it go. If you don't know precisely how to speak to yourself, think about how you'd talk to a dear friend who was struggling, doubting, and needing encouragement. Now use those exact words and tone with yourself.

Change can elicit fear. But the close cousin of fear is excitement. A part of you craves excitement and enjoys being afraid. That's why you go on rollercoasters, travel to new places, try new foods, meet new people, etc. Yet you simultaneously crave predictability and the constant. That's why you enjoy the prospect of climbing into your bed when you're tired, having the same Sunday evening meal, or seeing old friends.… Not everything should or ought to change. Change can be scary. Change can be exciting. Ask yourself what you want to change. You will probably have better success if you have a companion to make that change journey with you. Remember, God is there for you. Now take that first small step.

Next Steps …

- Without beating yourself up, ask what areas in your life you want to change. It's okay if you have lofty goals, but you must start small and slowly. If, for instance, you think your life is a mess physically and mentally, commit to making your bed first thing in the morning. Make that your habit for a month. Expand the order from there.

- It's good not to go it alone. Is there someone in your life to whom you can be accountable? Better yet, will they make the change with you? You don't have to have the exact change goals. Agree that you will be that daily encouragement.

- Write your goal down on paper or a post-it note. Could you keep it in front of you? Commit to taking one small step each day. It's okay if the step is tiny. You want to create a habit that you will sustain. You are more likely to succeed if the changing practice is doable.

- As you write out your goals, also write out potential setbacks and how you will address them. It's easy to imagine how you'll feel when you reach your goal. Now, how will you speak to yourself when you're down? This will be the difference between making a change or continuing life as usual.

4

GUILT AND SHAME
(BUT MORE ABOUT GUILT)

YOU PROBABLY DON'T WANT TO FEEL GUILT AND SHAME. You may not even want to read about it. I don't blame you. However, there is an important distinction to be made between the two. And without guilt, civilization would crumble. And with too much shame, you will crumble. So, what is the difference between the two, and why is guilt necessary?

For this book, I will not offer a profound theological explanation of guilt and how and why Jesus became the ultimate sacrifice as compensation for our transgressions—there are many excellent books written on this crucial topic. My emphasis is to draw a distinction between guilt and shame from a psychological point of view—and the difference is profound! But please indulge this non-theologian a moment to speak briefly on the theological understanding of guilt.

Guilt is the sense that you've screwed up or done something wrong. However, you don't have to run from the idea that you've blown it. The Apostle Paul reminds you in Romans chapter 3, WE ALL HAVE! We've all missed the mark. You can take some solace in knowing that you're not alone. You have plenty of company!

Paul's point in his epistle to the Romans is that you can never do enough good to earn salvation. That's why God stepped in and paid the price that you could never pay. Jesus's sacrifice on the cross was the one act bridging the chasm between how we've separated our lives from God through our sin and how He alone could make atonement for our sin.

However, this doesn't mean guilt no longer plays a beneficial role in your life. If we are to love, as God commands, we must be aware of how our actions impact others. But back to the difference between guilt and shame ...

Guilt is an awareness that you may have hurt someone else. It looks out toward others and sees how your actions have influenced them negatively. Guilt, then, can act as a correction tool.

Here's a guilt flow chart I just now made up:

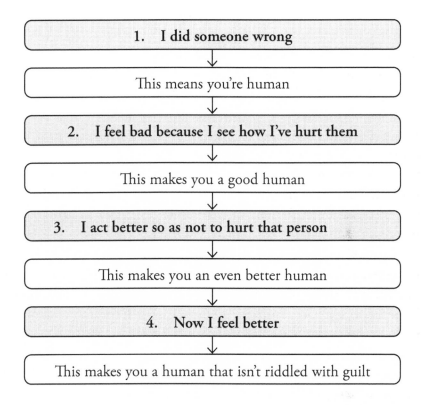

God's two most important commands are to love Him and love others as we love ourselves (Matt. 22). You don't have to be unduly weighed down with guilt to love others. Still, to love others, you must ask yourself how your actions, or lack thereof, impact other people's lives. And when you recognize that you have fallen short, you feel bad (guilt) and can course correct.

A Chinese saying goes: "If you want happiness for an hour, take a nap. If you want happiness for a day, go fishing. If you want happiness for a year, inherit a fortune. If you want happiness for a lifetime, help somebody."

We sometimes think we need to do more for ourselves to feel good. No research supports that happiness can be achieved by living just for yourself, doing whatever you want. (No guilt.) Even secular research supports the idea that we are happier and live fuller and more meaningful lives when we live, give, and sacrifice for others. And that is the message of the Gospel!

Through MRI technology, we see that giving activates the same brain parts stimulated by food and sex.[1] (My brain just made about thirty-seven jokes, but I'll restrain myself.) Altruism, it seems, is a part of our nature. Again, that's why we feel bad when we act against our nature, which is to love God and others. We feel guilt.

Numerous studies demonstrate that giving makes us happy, even happier than when we give to ourselves.[2] Research published in the Journal of Social Psychology indicates how doing good can minimize feelings of guilt and have the opposite effect and make you happy.[3]

Researchers in Great Britain had participants take a survey measuring life satisfaction, assigning all 86 participants to one of three groups. One group was instructed to perform a daily act of kindness for the next ten days. Another group was told to do something new every day over those ten days. A third group received no instructions. I'd fit well into this last group as I'm generally averse to reading instructions. However, I do not recommend that you follow my lead in this area.

After ten days, the researchers asked the participants to complete the life satisfaction survey again.

[1] Berridge KC, Kringelbach ML. Pleasure systems in the brain. Neuron. 2015 May 6;86(3):646-64. doi: 10.1016/j.neuron.2015.02.018. PMID: 25950633; PMCID: PMC4425246.

[2] Research article First published online February 3, 2014
Prosocial Spending and Happiness: Using Money to Benefit Others Pays Off Elizabeth W. Dunn, Lara B. Aknin, and Michael I. Norton View all authors and affiliations /Volume 23, Issue 1 /https://doi.org/10.1177/0963721413512503

[3] Ford BQ, Lam P, John OP, Mauss IB. The psychological health benefits of accepting negative emotions and thoughts: Laboratory, diary, and longitudinal evidence. J Pers Soc Psychol. 2018 Dec;115(6):1075-1092. doi: 10.1037/pspp0000157. Epub 2017 Jul 13. PMID: 28703602; PMCID: PMC5767148.

The survey found that the groups that practiced kindness and engaged in novel acts experienced a considerable happiness boost; the third group didn't get any happier. (Note to self: start reading instructions.) The findings suggest good deeds make us happier. And keep in mind that this boost in happiness came after only ten days of being kind. Can you imagine the positive impact of dedicating your life to giving?

But that's not all! According to another study published online in the Journal of Happiness Studies and conducted by researchers at Harvard Business School and the University of British Columbia, the happier participants felt about their past generosity, the more likely they were in the present to choose to spend time focused on someone else instead of themselves.[4] Here's the kicker, however. Not everyone remembered their giving happily. The ones who did, however, were overwhelmingly more likely to be even more giving.

This makes me think of Paul's famous writing in 1 Corinthians 13. You've probably heard this at weddings, if not at a regular church service. And the message is vital because it addresses how we are to act and the spirit with which we are to act. Paul writes:

"If I speak in human and angelic tongues but do not have love, I am a resounding gong or a clashing cymbal. And if I have the gift of prophecy and comprehend all mysteries and all knowledge; if I have all faith so as to move mountains but do not have love, I am nothing. If I give away everything I own, and if I hand my body over so that I may boast but do not have love, I gain nothing" (1 Cor. 13:1-3).

Marriage work is often the most rewarding—and challenging—of the thousands and thousands of hours of therapy I've offered. I believe in it passionately because marriage and family are important to God and our general welfare and happiness. And here's how Paul's important message above sometimes plays out in the therapy room:

[4] See Whillans AV, Dunn EW, Smeets P, Bekkers R, Norton MI. Buying time promotes happiness. Proc Natl Acad Sci U S A. 2017 Aug 8;114(32):8523-8527. doi: 10.1073/pnas.1706541114. Epub 2017 Jul 24. PMID: 28739889; PMCID: PMC5559044.

Joe: *"So tell me about this week."*

Man (folded arms): *"I did what you suggested, Joe. I sacrificed for my wife and took her to some crappy movie...."*

Wife: A somewhat angry face and tears forming.

The man continues: *"These women talked and talked about their feelings for over two hours, and not one person blasted off into space, not one bad guy was taken down.... And did I mention I blew about $25 on popcorn and a soda?"*

Wife: Tears now flow freely.

Joe: I look at the wife with sympathy....

Although this is only a mild exaggeration, the point is it's not just what we do, but the spirit with which we do the doing. You can give, but it won't increase your happiness or minimize guilty feelings unless you share freely and lovingly. But when love accompanies the giving, you not only fulfill God's command, but you create a positive feedback loop. The giving becomes more abundant and frequent and creates joy for both the recipient of your giving and you! A love that goes on and on and on ...

Shame is different from guilt. Whereas guilt says I've done bad, shame says I am bad. If you believe that you're no good (and that's a lie), you will have no motivation to change. "What's the point?" you will say. "It's just who I am." Shame breeds only misery and does not foster growth, change, and giving, as does appropriate guilt.

Remember, you are God's most magnificent creation. You are made in His image and likeness (Genesis 1).

Shame tends to be a self-fulfilling prophecy. Again, remember what Jesus said to the two blind men: "Become what you believe" (Matt. 9). They believed Jesus could heal them, and that's what they experienced. But conversely, if you feel unlovable (shame), you will not seek out loving relationships and may give up trying to lead a moral life. (We'll explore how and why you may be carrying shame in the next chapter.) Shame, which says I am bad, unworthy, unlovable, etc., is a destructive belief and should not be confused with guilt.

There are many outcomes of feeling shame. None are particularly good. Some, for example, have a narcissistic personality disorder and can be wildly successful on a worldly level: achieve great status, power, financial success, etc. But do not envy them. On the inside, they are likely miserable, feeling insecure and unlovable. Shame.

Additionally, they can lose the capacity to feel guilt and thus have no impetus to change their lives. They cannot truly love because they cannot see others as distinct from their wants and needs. In other words, they lack empathy.

Guilt has a bad reputation. Feelings of guilt may be your body telling you you've behaved badly. Use your head and heart and investigate your life. If you're acting in ways contradictory to what you believe is right and good, then change the behavior. Your guilt should subside as your conduct becomes consistent with what is right and true.

Sometimes, however, you may be so plagued with guilt that you feel bad no matter your behavior. So why is that, and what can you do about it? After taking your Next Steps, read on, and we'll explore....

Next Steps ...

- When someone accuses you of acting badly, how do you respond? Are you defensive? Do you reflect on what they say and see areas in your life for improvement?

- Which people in your life do you need to ask for forgiveness?

- How must you behave differently so that you lessen your sense of guilt?

- No matter how many good things you do, do you still always feel bad?

- Have you internalized a sense of "I am bad" (shame) or "I've done bad" (guilt)? We will explore this more deeply in the next chapter.

5

SHAME AND GUILT
(BUT MORE ABOUT SHAME)

IN THE LAST CHAPTER, I EXPLAINED HOW GUILT COULD BE more or less a force for good. Now I'll go more deeply into shame, where it comes from, and how to move beyond it. By the way, that's the tricky part. And you do want to move beyond it because it is a destructive force probably causing you misery. Shame can shape every aspect of your life, including how you see yourself as unworthy of love, joy, a sense of accomplishment, and nearly any of the good things God and life offer you.

A simple test of whether you are feeling appropriate guilt or bogged down with shame is this: It is guilt if you've done wrong, feel bad about it, use it as motivation to change and do good, and then feel better. The last part, about feeling better, IS KEY! Because if you feel bad no matter what you do, then it's probably shame. So where did you pick up this darkness? How can you experience the shift change required to love, be loved, and feel appropriately good about yourself? At the risk of sounding *psychobabbly*, let's talk about your childhood and *earlier*....

It is pretty common knowledge that a baby in the womb is affected by their mother's eating habits, nutrition, responses to stress, etc. While in the womb, you enjoyed about nine months of touch. Nice. But what happens immediately after birth can be another story.

Skin-to-skin contact between mother and child in the first hour after delivery helps regulate the baby's temperature, heart rate, and breathing and helps them cry less. It also increases the mother's relaxation hormones. In other words, our relationship quality matters from the beginning.

Touch is the first sense to develop, and babies use it to begin understanding their bodies and world. As reported in Scientific

American, by ages six to twelve, levels of the stress hormone cortisol were still much higher in children who had lived in orphanages for more than eight months[1] than in those who were adopted at or before the age of four months, according to a study from Development and Psychopathology. But you didn't have to grow up in an orphanage to experience deprivation. All along your early life's journey, you took in the information, and your brain either correctly or sometimes incorrectly formed an opinion about yourself and the world in which you live.

Did your caretaker respond to you when you became afraid? If not, you may have learned that your feelings don't matter. Did your dad congratulate you when you first managed to get some peas into your mouth instead of your hair? If not, you may have begun to believe that your accomplishments don't matter. Were you given adequate food when you were hungry? If not, you may think that your body and needs don't count.... *I don't matter* becomes the internal set point — shame.

Both good and bad memories last into adulthood if connected with powerful childhood emotions. If there are no strong emotions, events tend to be forgotten, but if coupled with high emotions, either good or bad, they are more likely to be remembered and influential.

Not all negative messages you received were due to deliberate neglect. Probably most were unintentional. You were afraid of the thunderstorm, but your parents didn't hear your cry because of the noise of the thunderstorm. Whose fault is it you now don't trust your spouse to meet your needs when you feel vulnerable? You probably don't make the connection to childhood, of course. You don't know

[1] How Important Is Physical Contact with Your Infant?
Author: Katherine Harmon
Publication: Scientific American
Publisher: SCIENTIFIC AMERICAN, a Division of Springer Nature America, Inc.
Date: May 6, 2010
Copyright © 2010, Scientific American, Inc.

that this sense of distrust began long before you even met your spouse. "I'm all alone, unworthy of being cared for," you believe. Shame.

It's easy to get judgmental about your parents and the misery you feel they caused you in childhood and extending into your adult life. But I want you to keep a few things in mind: first, most parents did their best. Certainly not all—but most. They had their trauma from childhood which shaped and made them into the parents they were to you.

Although I've indeed forgiven, I will not forget hearing from my mother, "Shame on you," when I had somehow messed up or disobeyed. I firmly believe she intended to correct my errant behavior, not instill a sense of shame. The pain I saw in her eyes wasn't so much about what I had done but came from some place deeper within her. I didn't understand this at the time. But later, as an adult, it became more apparent when I spoke to her about her childhood.

Her family was poor and living in Chicago. She recalled being sent to bed early some days. Why? Her parents didn't have enough food to feed her and her siblings supper. At one point, she shared a one-room apartment with her two brothers and parents. She recalled watching the family car repossessed—with her father's only winter coat inside. She cried all day. As her father struggled with alcoholism her parents were sometimes unavailable to her. Despair. What messages did she interpret about her place in the world? That it was unsafe? Uncaring? Fragile? Unforgiving? That she was undeserving? And how did those beliefs shape her parenting style? I don't think she wanted to share the shame she felt. But at times, she projected what she felt about herself onto me. It wasn't intentional—it came out of her sense of shame.

She also taught me invaluable and life-affirming lessons. She taught me compassion, love, and faith; she gave me the gift of laughter … I could go on and on and speak about the good she gave me. But for now, our focus is on shame and maybe where you developed it.

What were you "taught" about feelings when you were told, "big boys or girls don't cry?" Or told that you were spoiled because you wanted to go to Disneyland? You had to do the brown bag lunch when all your friends got to buy it? How much praise did your parents offer, fearful that you might become haughty? Maybe they withheld nurturing, wanting to teach you toughness.

If you're not sure about what went into forming your parents' life, ask them about *their* childhood. Did they have enough to eat? How were they loved? How did their sense of shame get passed down to you?

Up to this point, we've only explored how you may have inherited shame through unintentional acts. But what about those specific, harmful, traumatic acts?

Were you sexually or physically abused or neglected? And now, perhaps, one part of you understands you weren't to blame. But your sensory memory, where you hold memories in your body with emotion and felt sense, tells you something different. (More about that later.)

One client of mine years ago was repeatedly and horribly abused: Raped by a neighbor, not believed by her parents, and later told it was her fault, saying she was being sexually promiscuous; her babysitter abused her ... I could go on detailing the abuse. I won't. And although none of the abuse was her fault, period, decades later, she couldn't believe otherwise. After several suicide attempts (and anxiety off the charts) her sense of shame was so profound that she couldn't accept a free five-cent piece of candy from my office. Why? Shame.

You might rightly say, "That didn't happen to me, Joe. So why do I feel unworthy of love, dignity, etc.?" Good question.

Research supports the idea that the minor little traumas, some of which I talked about earlier in this chapter, add up and can be more destructive to our sense of self than single, more prominent forms of trauma. It is well known that childhood trauma can cause you to feel shame, but any mental health disorder that involves self-criticism or judgment can also cause it. Trying to live up to your perfectionistic standards can cause it. Because then every flaw tells you that you're not enough. Public humiliation and bullying can cause shame—bullying. The list, unfortunately, seems endless. And so you begin to hide and withdraw from others. Yet, the quality of our relationships most supports our mental health and a sense of, "I'm enough, I'm lovable."

But recovering from shame isn't just about feeling good. Shame can lead to addiction, depression, anxiety, and suicidal ideation. It may cause compulsive or excessive behaviors like strict dieting and *workaholism*. It can lead to mistrust issues making relationships nearly impossible. I could go on and on about the causes and fallout of shame, but more importantly, how do you recover from shame?

The first step is identifying where your shame comes from and how it impacts your life. How and when is your shame triggered?

This is no easy process, but perhaps you begin to explore what you *really* believe about yourself: Do you think you are evil? Unlovable? Don't matter? Unforgivable? You don't belong? Do you have difficulty trusting? Can you connect?

I want to offer some practical solutions to heal from shame, but honestly, don't look for a quick fix. This is a mountain climb, not a walk around the block. This may be a process when you decide it might be best to get some help from a professional therapist.

Shame may have begun because you were mistreated. But it will continue if you continue to mistreat yourself. In other words, you must start to have some compassion for yourself. Remember Jesus's words, "love others as you love yourself." It may be easier to begin by asking how you'd speak to a dear friend who had been abused. What words would you use with him? How would you talk to her? What would be your tone? How would you demonstrate compassion for their suffering? Meditate a moment on this. Got it? *Now, this is how you must begin to speak to and treat yourself!*

Neuroscience research shows that, like other habits, the more we engage in specific thoughts and behaviors, the more likely they become automatic and pervasive. But here's the beautiful thing: Your thoughts are not a permanent fixture of your personality—they can change. You can grow. How and what you think and feel about yourself is not a constant. The term for this is "plasticity." The saying, you can't teach an old dog new tricks is simply wrong!

God has called you to a life of growth and change. You don't have to stop learning once you graduate from college or you retire. While God gives you breath, you can change. This is the science. It is not my opinion.

Slow down. Listen. What is your inner dialogue? Remember the earlier example I gave when I challenged you with the question, "Is rejection painful?" The words you are speaking to yourself likely reinforce the belief of your lack of worth. You are supporting the shame.

Just become aware of the inner dialogue without judging it. Remember the powerful story when Jesus met the woman caught in adultery told in John 8?

"… the scribes and the Pharisees brought a woman who had been caught in adultery and made her stand in the middle. They said to him, 'Teacher, this woman was caught in the very act of committing adultery. Now in the law, Moses commanded us to stone such women. So what do you say?' They said this to test him so that they could have some charge to bring against him. Jesus bent down and began to write on the ground with his finger. But when they continued asking him, he straightened up and said to them, 'Let the one among you who is without sin be the first to throw a stone at her.' Again he bent down and wrote on the ground. And in response, they went away one by one, beginning with the elders. So he was left alone with the woman before him. Then Jesus straightened up and said to her, 'Woman, where are they? Has no one condemned you?' She replied, 'No one, sir.' Then Jesus said, 'Neither do I condemn you. Go, [and] from now on do not sin anymore.'" (John 8:3-11).

A few of thoughts … First, what happened to the dude? I'm guessing he was also captured if she was caught in the act. But she stood alone in front of the crowd where her sin was publicly addressed. Shame.

Second, what she did *was* wrong, but Jesus's focus was not on reinforcing the shame. He just wrote in the sand. His focus was on compassion, forgiveness, and change. Treat yourself similarly.

Third, Jesus didn't get into the blame game. He didn't point out everyone else's sin—including her accusers. You don't have to react to other people, although this can be extraordinarily difficult when you feel you're being attacked. You must take responsibility for your reactions, emotions, and words. Blame rarely changes hearts, minds, or behavior. Stop blaming yourself and others. Blame is only going to serve to keep you stuck and feeling resentful.

An interesting example of this is in scripture: Jesus is walking with His disciples when they see a blind man. They don't ask Jesus to heal the man or provide him comfort; they ask him instead whose fault it was that he was born blind. Was it his parents or his sin? Jesus pointed out that they were way off base. He responded by telling them to stop the blame game. Look instead for what God can do. He then healed the blind man. (John 9).

And fourth, and most important, Jesus did not condemn the woman caught in adultery, but instead offered forgiveness and a redo. Go and sin no more, He said. It's time to allow yourself to experience forgiveness and the opportunity to experience new life. Stop beating yourself up. You must begin to cultivate an inner voice that offers you compassion. Love others as you love yourself. It's God's command. So, what might this look like?

As a therapist, I frequently use EMDR (Eye Movement Desensitization and Reprocessing) therapy to help people process trauma and hurt. EMDR recognizes that the brain can constantly learn and take your experience and update it with current information. Why is this important? As I mentioned, you internalize messages about yourself and your world throughout your lifetime. And those past emotionally charged experiences—those experiences that cause you shame and anxiety, etc.—are charged. All those charged emotions interfere with your brain's updating process. You get stuck. You're emotionally reactive. You now respond to your life with all the emotional energy you felt when traumatized. It keeps you from thinking with the parts of your brain that are healthy and mature. Again, remember that I'm not necessarily referring to major traumas but all the little messages that add to your feeling of shame.

The therapist helps guide the client through rapid eye movement to help update those early disturbing memories, like what you do during REM (rapid eye movement) sleep. This sleep pattern allows you to process troubling events. An alternative to eye movement is tapping. After brief sets of eye movements or tapping, the therapist checks in with the client and asks what they notice. Although the process is more complicated than what I'm explaining here, EMDR efficiently and effectively allows the brain to update dysfunctional thinking and memory with more adaptive thoughts.

EMDR helps you to break through where you're stuck so you can enjoy the healthy life you want. If you're really stuck or highly reactive, I strongly suggest getting professional help, preferably from a trained therapist in EMDR. However, what are some practical steps if you're not in a place to do that? How can you allow your brain to update itself?

I think you might enjoy this process. What do you need? Maybe some comfortable outdoor shoes, access to the outdoors (the prettier, the better), and an open mind. Let's take a walk ...

Your first question is, "Joe, why are we outside?"

I could fill the following 200 pages with research supporting nature's psychological and physical health benefits. But luckily for both of us, I've chosen not to do this and will instead give a few highlights. Ready?

Research has shown that spending time in nature can improve memory, lower stress hormones and blood pressure, reduce feelings of depression and anxiety, enhance immune system functioning, increase self-esteem, help with self-control, improve working memory and cognitive flexibility, replenish mental resources, increase happiness, help the brain deal with eating disorders, positively affect mood disorders[2], buffer the effects of loneliness and isolation, help develop a sense of purpose and meaning in life, and finally, it's just sometimes fun to get dirty while playing outside. Okay. All of the above is based on research except the messy part. That might be just me who enjoys that.

Research has also shown that just looking at pictures of nature and listening to its sounds has beneficial effects.[3] But let's go for the real thing.

Now, I want you outside, and perhaps it would be good to have another warm body with you instead of the imaginary Joe Sikorra—because what I'm going to ask you to do can cause distress. However, if you are with another person, you are not to check in with them about their memory of events that you may have shared. Why? Two primary reasons: One, memory is faulty, and everyone will remember things differently. And two, it is about your interpretation of what happened and how it affected *you*. Two people can share the same experience, like a movie, but walk away with an entirely different understanding.

Now that you're moving your body in nature, go ahead and ask yourself what disturbing memories (maybe from childhood) are feeding your distress, sense of shame, anxiety, etc.

Is there an image that goes along with that memory? How disturbing is it? It might even be helpful to rate the disturbance of the memory on a scale from 1 to 10. Why? Because after each time you do this exercise, you can rate your level of distress again. If you find that you're less distressed, then you're onto something!

[2] See Brown DK, Barton JL, Gladwell VF. Viewing nature scenes positively affects recovery of autonomic function following acute-mental stress. Environ Sci Technol. 2013 Jun 4;47(11):5562-9. doi: 10.1021/es305019p. Epub 2013 May 16. PMID: 23590163; PMCID: PMC3699874.

[3] See Franco LS, Shanahan DF, Fuller RA. A Review of the Benefits of Nature Experiences: More Than Meets the Eye. Int J Environ Res Public Health. 2017 Aug 1;14(8):864. doi: 10.3390/ijerph14080864. PMID: 28763021; PMCID: PMC5580568.

Now, ask what negative beliefs you have about yourself because of that experience. Do you believe that what happened to you is your fault? That you're a terrible person? Are you unlovable? Unworthy? This is the tricky part of the exercise because part of you might say, "No. I'm lovable or ..." But another deeper part doesn't quite believe in the good.

Allow yourself to be honest. It might hurt. But remember what God says: "You will know the truth, and the truth will set you free" (John 8:32).

As you continue to walk and process, notice how your brain begins to feed you with current, more adaptive information. You were a child. It wasn't your fault. Notice the evidence that you are lovable. Good. Safe. At this time, you can also allow yourself to reflect on God's messages of love. God created you in His image (Gen. 1:27); He formed you in your mother's womb (Psalm 139:13); you are loved, and God calls you His friend (John 15). Allow yourself to feel good and believe in the good.

Now go ahead and imagine future challenges, but now picture yourself dealing effectively with these challenges. Not reacting negatively with shame or anger, but with love, calm, and assurance. Baseball players or golfers don't mentally rehearse striking out or hitting the ball into the pond, as I frequently do. They "see" themselves and rehearse success.

Keep in mind that the early Apostles blew it. A lot. But they grew. God's love transformed their lives—and so can yours! The very same Spirit that God gave them He gives you now! You weren't meant to do this alone. You can't. But with God, all things are possible (Matt. 19)!

Let go of the shame.

Next Steps ...

- Get outside. Move. Now while you do this, can you identify your early life experiences where you may have begun to internalize shame? Speak honestly. What do you believe about yourself? That you're unlovable? No good? Are you at fault? Now also speak about what you'd prefer to believe about yourself as you continue your outdoor moving journey. Would you like to believe that you are lovable? Have you done the best you could? Not to blame? As you walk, allow yourself to process. If you get stuck in a negative feedback loop, ask yourself how you would speak to a little boy or girl if they were in the position you had been placed in as a child. Use this same compassion, tone, and understanding with yourself. Again, this can be a challenging exercise. If it becomes overwhelming or doesn't seem helpful, consider getting help from a professional therapist.

- How do you speak to yourself when you are struggling? Are you harsh with yourself? Become aware of your self-talk. How do you talk to yourself when you make a mistake? When don't you know what to do? When do you feel rejected? If you consistently beat yourself up, it's time to practice a more affirming tone with yourself. How you speak to yourself and the words you use matter a lot! If it's initially too difficult to form more positive self-talk, imagine how a loving friend, either real or imagined, or Jesus himself would speak to you. Let that voice of love become what you hear.

- How do you treat others because of your sense of shame? Do you project your hurt onto them? It's not uncommon for people to do this. Remember the Golden Rule: treat others as you want to be treated. Slow yourself down from reacting with anger at yourself or others. Chances are that you react based on fears and messages you internalized long ago. Cultivate forgiveness. Forgive yourself and others as soon as possible. Live with compassion and love for yourself and others.

• What words and actions would help you make positive life changes? As you cultivate more positive self-talk, reinforce it with small, loving steps toward yourself and others. As the saying goes, be the change you want to see in the world.

6

ANXIETY AND CONTROL

M Y SON, BENJAMIN, IS BLIND. BUT THAT DOESN'T mean that he shouldn't learn how to drive. Right?

"I got this, Dad. Let go," as his hand brushed up against mine while making a left turn.

"Oh, I know. Sorry."

The steering wheel got a little crowded with my hands at ten and two and his left hand reaching across from the passenger seat. I have to be more careful, I thought. He was so confident. So sure of himself—and so I maintained the illusion. As far as he was concerned, he was making it all happen.

"Slow down!" I yelled. "You're going way too fast for this turn!"

I slammed on the brakes, then hit the gas, jerking the car, throwing our bodies forward, and then back into our seats. Of course, our "sports car," an underpowered four-cylinder Subaru, didn't have rocket-like power. Still, I compensated by using its excellent braking to create the illusion of a wild and fast ride.

He started laughing. I laughed because he made me feel funny.

Usually, after a couple of hours, he'd take his hand off the wheel without notice if we were on a long drive.

"Go ahead, Dad, you drive for a while. My hand is tired."

"What?" I'd say. "I was just falling asleep."

Ben and I repeated this routine almost daily, nearly everywhere we drove. He felt good about himself.

It hit me, probably on one of my longer drives with Ben, that you and I probably live with a similar illusion. We're driving the car. And we just don't recognize that we, too, are blind. We think we see so clearly. And this illusion makes us feel safe. Competent. In charge.

"I know what I'm doing, God. And this is what I want *you* to do, Maker of the Universe...."

Like Ben, who thinks he drives us safely to our destination, it feels good. And as a loving father, I don't want to destroy the illusion. But what does God think about our illusion of control?

We don't suspect it, but I think God is driving the car. We believe we are doing it all with one hand on the wheel of life. And so we focus on all the wrong things. As we maintain the illusion of control, we need not exercise trust. And if the breaks all go our way and the future seems secure, we feel great—no anxiety. Life, it seems, is in control. Our control.

But what happens when we get a couple of cracks in our armor of illusion, and we recognize we don't have control, and our faith isn't strong enough to find comfort in our trust in God? Anxiety. Fear sets in.

If we focused on the fact that at any minute, our lives could end abruptly (and that is a fact) we'd constantly feel anxiety—so we wisely choose not to focus too much on that. Perhaps if we recognized that we were made for eternity, and this life is just preparation for the next, we'd be okay with our fragility.

We must take action on the things we can control, yet simultaneously come to terms with the fact that much of what will happen to us in life is out of our control. However, trust in God will continue to keep us steady. We must act and trust. This is the antidote for anxiety.

I believe there is ample evidence of God and His absolute care and love for you and me. I'm not a scientist, but look at the majesty of creation in which we live. An accident? And the unbelievable miracle of life itself? Random chance? I don't think so.

The Apostle Paul says it this way: "Ever since the creation of the world, his invisible attributes of eternal power and divinity have been able to be understood and perceived in what he has made...." (Romans 1:20).

Look around, and you will be reminded of *The One* by witnessing His creation.

Although we can certainly make a mess of things, creation is perfect—and God has an ideal plan for you. To believe this is to trust. And trust is a choice. All along your life, you will have to trust and choose to act.

In my clinical practice, I've never seen such high rates of anxiety and stress. Another way to say this is that I've never seen so many people afraid. But we usually don't like to tell our friends, or therapists, that we're scared. Anxiety sounds more adult and acceptable—but maybe we should rethink this.

While depression is the condition most people associate with mental health issues, it is not the leading cause of disability worldwide—it is anxiety.

What are some of the symptoms? Apprehension (worrying about a dark future), feeling edgy and irritable, difficulties with concentrating, muscle tension, headaches, trembling, inability to relax, lightheaded-ness, sweating, rapid heart rate, rapid breathing (not due to working out), pain in the upper abdomen, dizziness, and dry mouth. These are just a few of the symptoms. Do any of these symptoms look familiar?

Some research indicates that heavy stress can shorten your life by almost three years.[1] In other words, our bodies take a huge hit.

Research also shows that stress results in accidents, absenteeism, employee turnover, diminished productivity, and direct medical, legal,

[1] National Institute for Health and Welfare. "Heavy stress and lifestyle can predict how long we live." ScienceDaily. www.sciencedaily.com/releas-es/2020/03/200311100857.htm (accessed February 9, 2023).

and insurance bills costing the United States $300 billion annually.[2] And you think therapy is expensive?

Stress, fear, anxiety, or whatever you want to call it, also threatens your relationships. It causes you to be more withdrawn and distracted and less affectionate. You take less time for pleasurable activities with those you love.

Stress can lead you to feel angrier. It can also lead to depression. If you're constantly worried that things won't work out, you can begin to feel hopeless.

Stress isn't a 21st-century phenomenon. God spoke about it in Scripture thousands of years ago. The most significant difference between now and then is that we have a clearer picture of its impact on our bodies, and we can use fancy words and codes to describe it. God usually uses the word "fear," but we give Generalized Anxiety

[2] [1] Hoel, H., Sparks, K., & Cooper, C. (2001). The cost of Violence/Stress at work and the benefits of a violence/stress-free working environment. International Labour Organisation.

[2] National Institute for Occupational Safety and Health (NIOSH). Stress At Work Booklet. Publication No. 99-101.

[3] Flash, What is the cost of employee turnover? Compensation & Benefits Review, Sept/Oct 1997: Article #8582, 1998.

[4] NIOSH. Costs of absenteeism, cited 2002, available from http://hr.cch. com/default.asp

[5] Munce, S. E., Stansfeld, S.A., Blackmore, E.R., & Stewart, D. E. (2007). The role of depression and chronic pain conditions in absenteeism: Results from a national epidemiologic survey. Journal of Occupational Environmental Medicine, 49(11), 1206-1211. (PubMed)

[6] Druss, B. G., Rosenheck, R. A., & Sledge, W. H. (2000) Health and disability costs of depressive illness in a major U.S. corporation. American Journal of Psychiatry, 157(8), 1274-1278. (PubMed)

[7] Johnston, K., Westerfield, W., Momin, S., Phillippi, R., & Naidoo, A. (2009). The direct and indirect costs of employee depression, anxiety, and emotional disorders: An employer case study. Journal of Occupational Environmental Medicine, 51(5), 564-577. (PubMed)

[8] Perkins, A. (1994) Saving money by reducing stress. Harvard Business Review, 72(6), 12.

Disorder a code: ICD-10 CODE: F41.1. Or, if you want a little more info, ICD-CODE F41.1 is a billable ICD-10 code used for healthcare diagnosis reimbursement of Generalized Anxiety Disorder. Its corresponding ICD-9 code is 300.02. There. You now know something that confuses me, too. And I have to use these codes! How about we go back to calling it fear and see what we can do about it!

Let's start with what God says about fear and how to address it. By the way, this is also consistent with sound psychological research. I'll explain.

"There is no fear in love, but perfect love drives out fear because fear has to do with punishment, and so one who fears is not yet perfect in love" (1 John 4:18). There is no room for fear (anxiety) in love. And God loves you completely! B-a-m!

Support and relationship help to combat fear. I won't bore you with research here. Instead, think of your own experiences to prove this point. When you were a child in bed and became afraid, whether it was because of the monster under your bed or the fierce thunderstorm, what did you do? You probably ran to your parents' room for assurance. We sometimes forget this vital antidote as adults—but it is the relationship that quiets the fear.

I remember my days as a cop and some scarier times, like when I was seriously outnumbered and my life was being threatened. There was nothing sweeter than the sound of sirens as my brothers and sisters in blue were responding to help. Whether you're a cop or teacher or the stock market goes down, whatever makes you afraid, you're meant to turn to those around you for support.

We frequently think of our primary relationships as our marriages and families. But there is a relationship that supersedes these extraordinary alliances: our connection with God. As strong as the union within marriage, our relationship with God alone is what lives in eternity.

"Jesus said to them, 'The children of this age marry and are given in marriage; but those who are deemed worthy to attain to the coming age and to the resurrection of the dead neither marry nor are given in marriage'" (Luke 20:34-35). Our most intimate relationship will be with God. Imagine! And this is eternal. When we experience this perfect love, there will be no room for fear!

You rightly may say, "But Joe, I still live here on planet Earth." True. That's why we continuously strengthen our faith and trust in God while stregthening our relationships here. God asks you to act. And you can take very doable steps to lower your life stress/fear/anxiety levels. To begin with, you must first address your focus.

Remember, anxiety is about your worry about what may or may not happen—emphasis on the future tense. Let me make an obvious point: you don't know what will happen, and you cannot live in the future—impossible. Yet that is where your anxiety lives! And frequently, when you feel this kind of fear, you look for control. Only it often doesn't work out too well. You try to control others, or you pull back and hide.

I recently worked with a client whom I admire greatly. Toward the end of our session, he said he felt great, at peace. "Nice," I replied. Then he said, "but I don't know what will happen." Future tense. And his anxiety went back up immediately.

Although what he said couldn't be more accurate, that is what we all face. You may get cancer, lose your job, a fire could ravish your house, etc. And you can either choose to worry about the future and the calamities that may or may not happen or focus on what is going on in your life. If you pulled yourself back into this moment, your anxiety would immediately decrease. This is not to say that your present circumstances may not also be challenging. But most of your anxiety concerns what may or may not happen, not what is in the moment.

Paul writes, "Have no anxiety at all, but in everything, by prayer and petition, with thanksgiving, make your requests known to God" (Phil. 4:6). Bring your requests to God *and do so with thanksgiving*. It is nearly impossible to feel afraid while simultaneously giving thanks. And when you pray, you strengthen your relationship with God, acknowledging that he will take care of you. You do not have to know precisely how God will provide for you. You're not in control. But you can choose to trust Him and recognize that although you may not understand His plan, He has one just for you!

Jesus says, "Therefore I tell you, do not worry about your life, what you will eat [or drink], or about your body, what you will wear. Is not life more than food and the body more than clothing? Look at the birds in the sky; they do not sow or reap, they gather nothing into barns, yet your heavenly Father feeds them. Are not you more important than they? Can any of you by worrying add a single moment to your lifespan? Why are you anxious about clothes? Learn from the way the wild-flowers grow. They do not work or spin. But I tell you that not even Solomon in all his splendor was clothed like one of them. If God so clothes the grass of the field, which grows today and is thrown into the oven tomorrow, will he not much more provide for you, O you of little faith? So do not worry and say, 'What are we to eat?' or 'What are we to drink?' or 'What are we to wear?' All these things the pagans seek. Your heavenly Father knows that you need them all. But seek first the kingdom [of God] and his righteousness, and all these things will be given you besides. Do not worry about tomorrow; tomorrow will take care of itself. Sufficient for a day is its own evil" (Matthew 6:25-34).

While we can look forward to eternity with God and the unfathomable blessings that await while we are here, God wants us to live in the here and now! He doesn't talk about your retirement or 401K; He says I have your back now!

Emotions are natural and instructive. And they can be pleasurable. Fear is an emotion, but not necessarily a pleasant one. And I think we can sometimes place too much emphasis on our feelings. They can make us aware of something important that may require us to take action. If, for instance, you are afraid about your relationship, your fear might indicate that the relationship needs attention. You can then explore what is wrong and take steps to remedy the problem. When you feel terrific about your relationships, it tells you that you are doing something right. If you are miserable in your job, it might mean that it's the wrong job for you, etc.

And fear, if put in its proper context, can also be good. When we face something new, it can feel like fear, but we can also channel that emotion into excitement. Rather than being too frightened, we can lean into it and use the energy it provides us. Even a new relationship can cause us fear. What if they don't like us? What if it doesn't work out? It's all possible. But you can use that energy to strengthen your desire, or you can use it to run.

There is a reason some of us love to go on wild roller-coasters —we like the excitement. If instead of calling what you feel *fear*, you choose to call it *excitement*, it can give you energy and life. You don't know what will happen. Fine. You can be afraid and feel the worry, or lean into it and treat it as exciting.

As I sit and write now, my mind wanders to thinking about my son, Ben. (I'm easily distracted.) Because of my deep love for him and his precarious health condition, he warrants the best I can give him. No one would blame me if I spoke extensively and lived in my worries and concerns about how to take care of him, how much longer he has to live, how I'll face his passing, etc. I could quickly become consumed with fear. But would that contribute to the betterment of either his or my life right now? Not really. Instead, I can acknowledge this reality and focus on lavishing him with love right now. I can share laughter and joy with him. This is the choice I make. You, too, can feel the fear, then redefine it as an opportunity and relish all the blessings found in the moment.

There is a big fancy word I love to throw around from time to time. I don't have many, so I use them judiciously. It's called "alexithymia." (Wow. Even my computer doesn't recognize the spelling. But it's a real word. Promise.) It means an inability to identify and differentiate one's feelings. And why is this so important? Because if you don't know what you're feeling, you are less able to take appropriate action. If this is you, don't worry. You can get better at identifying your feelings more accurately with practice.

There are slogans such as "No Fear." But this is a ridiculous idea. The bravest among us feel fear. The difference is that they try not to let it immobilize them—better to feel the fear and act anyway. Don't ignore it. Acknowledge it. Use it to make appropriate preparation, then act.

If you think about it, probably the most critical decisions and actions you've taken involved some level of fear. There was probably some fear associated with moving away to college, quitting your job to strike out on your own, or allowing yourself to fall in love.

Studies done with people near death reveal that they regret not risking more rather than taking a risk and failing. You'll unlikely approach your end with the words, "If only I had more money in the bank." But you might regret not risking falling in love or taking that backpacking trip across the country or ...

Risk, which involves fear, will allow you to experience more passion. God wants you to take chances. Jesus speaks about it in the parable of the ten coins:

"A nobleman went off to a distant country to obtain the kingship for himself and then to return. He called ten of his servants and gave them ten gold coins[e] and told them, 'Engage in trade with these until I return.' His fellow citizens, however, despised him and sent a delegation after him to announce, 'We do not want this man to be our king.' But when he returned after obtaining the kingship, he had the servants called, to whom he had given the money, to learn what they had gained by trading. The first came forward and said, 'Sir, your gold coin has earned ten additional ones.' He replied, 'Well done, good servant! You have been faithful in this very small matter; take charge of ten cities.' Then the second came and reported, 'Your gold coin, sir, has earned five more.' And to this servant, he said, 'You, take charge of five cities.' Then the other servant came and said, 'Sir, here is your gold coin; I kept it stored away in a handkerchief, for I was afraid of you, because you are a demanding person; you take up what you did not lay down and you harvest what you did not plant.' He said to him, 'With your own words I shall condemn you, you wicked servant.

You knew I was demanding, taking up what I did not lay down and harvesting what I did not plant; why did you not put my money in a bank? Then on my return I would have collected it with interest.' And to those standing by he said, 'Take the gold coin from him and give it to the servant who has ten.' But they said to him, 'Sir, he has ten gold coins.' 'I tell you, to everyone who has, more will be given, but from the one who has not, even what he has will be taken away. Now as for those enemies of mine who did not want me as their king, bring them here and slay them before me'" (Luke 19:12-27).

God doesn't want you to play it safe. We have all been given different talents and abilities, and we will be held to account for acting on what we've been given. Use your faith to quiet the fear, then act!

Next Steps …

- Make a list of the things you worry about. Then, for each worry item, list small steps you can take to improve the likelihood of a better outcome. Remember to keep the steps small. This will increase the chance of you taking action.

- Rate your anxiety on a scale of 1 to 10, with 1 being low anxiety and 10 being high. After ten minutes of taking action, as mentioned above, again rate your anxiety and notice how it decreases.

- Make a list of all the things you've worried about in the past, and ask yourself how it worked out. If, at this point, you recognize that the anxiety may have been unwarranted, ask yourself about your worries right now—perhaps they, too, will work out just fine.

- At least once a day, whether at mealtime with family or while you're by yourself, spend three minutes giving thanks to God for all your blessings. Again, notice how your anxiety decreases after just a few minutes of giving thanks.

- You may face tremendous obstacles, and you have no idea how to overcome them. Spend time in prayer. Acknowledge your fear, but then recognize that God's strength comes into its own in your weakness. His grace is all you need (2 Cor. 12). Give these worries to The One who is all-powerful.

- Spend a few minutes, several times a day, to breathe. If you can close your eyes and be outside while you do this, all the better. Breathe deep and slow. While you do this, become aware of what you hear and feel. Use your senses to bring yourself into the moment. Remember, most of your anxiety and fear aren't based on the moment but on the unknown future.

- Take your worry and redefine it as an opportunity. Shape that worry into something exciting and new that you get to experience.

7

SOCIAL MEDIA, MEDIA, AND ADDICTION

WHEN YOU HEAR THE WORD ADDICTION, MEDIA probably isn't the first thing that comes to mind. That's why I wanted to devote a chapter to it—it is destructive. The use of social media has seen an exponential rise in recent years. According to some recent research, the prevalence of social media addiction among social media users is almost 40%.[1]

You've undoubtedly experienced the value of social media: catching up with distant relatives or friends, sharing news, finding groups with common interests, sharing cute pictures of your pet iguana, etc. But since you probably understand how it serves and delights you, allow me to be the harbinger of the bad.

Due to its impact on the brain, social media is addictive both physically and psychologically. Some researchers have found that self-disclosure on social networking sites lights up the same part of the brain that fires up when taking an addictive substance.[2] Researchers also found that smartphone addiction can lead to an imbalance in brain chemistry.

[1] Ramesh Masthi NR, Pruthvi S, Phaneendra MS. A Comparative Study on Social Media Usage and Health Status among Students Studying in Pre-University Colleges of Urban Bengaluru. Indian J Community Med. 2018 Jul-Sep;43(3):180-184. doi: 10.4103/ijcm.IJCM_285_17. PMID: 30294084; PMCID: PMC6166494.

[2] Thomson K, Hunter SC, Butler SH, Robertson DJ. Social media 'addiction': The absence of an attentional bias to social media stimuli. J Behav Addict. 2021 Apr 13;10(2):302-313. doi: 10.1556/2006.2021.00011. PMID: 33852419; PMCID: PMC8996807.

You may not consider yourself an addict. But most addicts, whether addicted to alcohol, drugs, or porn, don't feel themselves addicts—until they try to go without.

When was the last time you set your phone or connected device down for an extended period? Was it difficult? Were you thinking about it while not using it? Did you feel anxious? These are signs you might be addicted.

Have you congratulated yourself for getting that automatic notification that says your media usage went down for that week? Then you read how many hours you were engaged and were somewhat shocked. Ten hours? Twenty? Forty? The global average time spent using social media platforms per day is 142 minutes in 2021.[3] Crazy! Would you like those hours back to do something more constructive with that time? I pray it doesn't happen, but when I reach the pearly gates or am faced with a life review, I don't want the Lord to say, "Wow. 146,426 hours online …" I don't think He'd have to say anything else. Message received. You can't recapture time gone by. But you can change how you use your time moving forward.

We are in an age where technology expands beyond what we can comprehend. We don't fully understand how it affects us, particularly on social media. But we do know some things. Trust me, those who create your favorite social media platforms, whether Twitter, Facebook, TikTok, other emerging A.I. technologies—or your favorite news outlet—know how to keep you "engaged." That's one of the words they use. It sounds so much more appealing than "addicted." But let's face it, when you or others around you use it compulsively or excessively, what else would you call it?

[3] Riehm KE, Feder KA, Tormohlen KN, Crum RM, Young AS, Green KM, Pacek LR, La Flair LN, Mojtabai R. Associations Between Time Spent Using Social Media and Internalizing and Externalizing Problems Among US Youth. JAMA Psychiatry. 2019 Dec 1;76(12):1266-1273. doi: 10.1001/jamapsychiatry.2019.2325. PMID: 31509167; PMCID: PMC6739732.

The simplest way to determine if you're abusing or addicted to social media is if you feel an uncontrollable urge to use it. Rather than opening up your favorite app, stop. Would you feel fine just putting your device down, or do you feel strongly pulled in? Are you spending time on your app and neglecting other important aspects of your life? Family time? Relationships? Exercise? Sleep? Prayer? It's not necessarily easy but look at how much time a day you spend on social media, and then ask yourself if that is the best use of your time. Are there better ways to spend those minutes, those hours?

Not to sound like that crotchety old guy, because really, I'm not there—yet. But I remember the first time I saw a group of teenagers sitting together. They were all staring at their phones. Silent. They were checking out their social media connections, liking each other's posts, etc. But scarcely a word was shared among them—the irony. But teens aren't the only culprits. Adults. Children. We are building a virtual world in which we seek connection—it does not compare with the real one.

When you access your favorite apps or hear the news alerts, dopamine, the pleasure chemical in your brain, says, "Oh yeah. That feels great." But just like alcohol, the pleasure lasts only so long. So back you go!

But it's not just your desire to connect—which is a healthy thing—that draws you back in. The creators of these apps lure you in with their bells, notifications, and alerts. We become like Pavlov's dogs: they smell meat and start to drool. (I do the same thing.) And although you probably don't drool, or at least try not to, your brain gets a little rush when you hear that you have notifications.

Social media's stated purpose was to help people connect. Ironically, however, you peruse your connections alone, see how wonderful everyone else's life appears, and feel more lonely than before—even if people surround you. So back you go to try and satiate that loneliness. It can become a downward spiral.

If I may suggest that you conduct your experiment to compare the value of social media connections versus real connections, try this: go ahead and spend two hours indulging in all your social media platforms. Take a ten-minute break, then rate your experience, happiness, and how your body feels on a scale of 1 to 10. Ten is great! I can't wait to do it again! One is not great at all. Now the second step of your research study: Grab a friend or a willing participant and go for a hike. Play hard. Have a meaningful conversation. Do almost anything that involves relationship, movement, laughter, etc. But NO devices are allowed! Now rate that experience, measuring your happiness, how your body feels, etc. Which was better?

According to research, excessive use of media can contribute to anxiety, depression, feelings of loneliness, suicidal ideation, eyestrain, and anger. It can lead to poorer cognitive performance and shrinking parts of the brain associated with maintaining attention[4]—just a partial list.

So if there are so many adverse effects to its excessive use, why do you get sucked in? Again, you may begin your foray into it for excellent reasons: You want to connect with others! Sweet! However, research suggests you may be more susceptible to it due to low self-esteem, personal dissatisfaction, depression and hyperactivity, and even a lack of affection.

There is speculation as to why exactly it can be so harmful. I want to keep to the basics. First, consciously or unconsciously, you are making private comparisons. Let's face it; you post what will make you look best. And others do the same. It tells a distorted and partial story only. But you can't help but look at what others are posting and think that you don't quite measure up. Children and teens are particularly susceptible. Image-based platforms like Instagram have very harmful effects on mental health, especially for teens struggling with body

[4] Yang X, Yip BHK, Mak ADP, Zhang D, Lee EKP, Wong SYS. The Differential Effects of Social Media on Depressive Symptoms and Suicidal Ideation Among the Younger and Older Adult Population in Hong Kong During the COVID-19 Pandemic: Population-Based Cross-sectional Survey Study. JMIR Public Health Surveill. 2021 May 25;7(5):e24623. doi: 10.2196/24623. PMID: 33835937; PMCID: PMC8153033.

image, anxiety, depression, and eating disorders. It leaves you feeling "less than." Making these kinds of comparisons can lead to envy and low self-esteem.

We all crave love. We want to be seen and heard. But we want to be loved for who we authentically are. Warts and all. Social media doesn't offer this. You post your best self and hope for a "like."

The apostle Paul addresses these themes in his letter to the Corinthians. Specifically, read 1 Corinthians, chapters 4 and 12. He managed how he was being compared to other apostles. He said he just didn't care about these comparisons. He didn't even rank himself among his peers. He knew that God's judgment alone was what mattered. In chapter 12, he expands and talks about the value of the Body of Christ. And as a Christian, you are an integral member of that body. Paul points out that it's silly for an eye to feel superior to the intestines. It is the organ that is not seen that, in all likelihood, has superior value. You can live without an eye or great hair, but life without a stomach?

You are a unique creation. You are a magnificent creation. Recognize that. Be what *you* were made to be, not envious or imitating someone else. But don't brag. You had nothing to do with your creation. You are, however, responsible for what you do with what you've been given. You give dignity and honor to your body and life by living out your function as a member of Christ's body.

It's easy to get caught up in what others are doing, what they're wearing, etc. You may want to stay up on everyone and everything for fear of missing out (FOMO). But I want to suggest rather boldly and bluntly, and I can only do this because Jesus said it first: "Therefore I tell you, do not worry about your life, what you will eat [or drink], or about your body, what you will wear. Is not life more than food and the body more than clothing? Look at the birds in the sky; they do not sow or reap, they gather nothing into barns, yet your heavenly Father feeds them. Are not you more important than they? Can any of you by worrying add a single moment to your life-span? Why are you anxious about clothes? Learn from the way the wildflowers grow. They do not work or spin. But I tell you that not even Solomon in all his splendor was clothed like one of them. If God so clothes the grass of the field, which grows today and is thrown into the oven tomorrow, will he not much more provide for you, O you of little faith? So do not worry and say, 'What are we to eat?' or 'What are we to drink?' or 'What are we to wear?' All these things the pagans seek. Your heavenly Father knows that you need them all. But seek first the kingdom [of God] and his righteousness, and all these things will be given you besides. Do not worry about tomorrow; tomorrow will take care of itself...." (Matthew 6:25-34).

The apostle Paul speaks about how you use your time this way: "But make sure that you don't get so absorbed and exhausted in taking care of all your day-by-day obligations that you lose track of the time and doze off, oblivious to God. The night is about over, dawn is about to break. Be up and awake to what God is doing! God is putting the finishing touches on the salvation work he began when we first believed. We can't afford to waste a minute, must not squander these precious daylight hours in frivolity and indulgence...." (Romans 13:11-14 The Message).

Get outside. By yourself. With others. With God. Connect with what matters most: God. Faith. Your real life.

I will address the news media only briefly. News organizations use all the same addicting tools as other social media outlets. The terrible news sucks you in. The breaking news keeps you excited. And depressed. And anxious. They know how to keep you sucked in. However, we are more divided than ever. News organizations exploit this and use it to their advantage—not yours. It has become an "Us versus Them" attack. We have political differences and divides. But you do not have to treat others you disagree with as your enemy. It's healthy to debate different ideas but not to attack the person. God says that we are brothers and sisters—we are family. And even if you thought of the other as your enemy. How would you treat them? Jesus is clear and adamant: "You have heard that it was said, 'You shall love your neighbor and hate your enemy.' But I say to you, love your enemies, and pray for those who persecute you" (Matthew 5:43-44).

Cutting your social media use down has been shown to minimize your risk of developing depression significantly. You may be using it to "kill time." But do you want to do that? You have only so many minutes and hours. Time is the most precious commodity you've been given. What do you really want to do with it?

Next Steps …

- Record how much time per week you're spending on social media. Write it down. Look at that number daily and ask yourself if it is the best use of your time.

- Consider deleting your social media apps from your smartphone. While you can still access them from your personal computer, keep them off your phone. It may help decrease the amount of time you spend on social media overall.

- Turn off your personal phone during work, school, meals, and during recreational activities. I strongly suggest keeping your phone out of the bedroom.

- Set aside a certain amount of time dedicated to social media per day. Turn on a timer to help keep you accountable.

- Take up a new hobby that's not technology related. Consider using half the time you currently devote to social media and devote it to a positive activity like exercise, prayer, or donating that time to a worthy charity.

8

ADDICTION

YOU UNDOUBTEDLY DIDN'T START OUT THINKING YOU'D become addicted. You probably started drinking or using because it felt good—it made you feel okay with yourself and the world. It "worked" for you. But now it's all changed. The good feelings are gone. Fun—gone. And you can no longer escape. A part of you may deny you're addicted. Most people do. You keep trying to get back the feelings "using" initially gave you. But it doesn't work.

Feel hopeless? Please don't. There is hope. There is another way.

The only reason I struggled with the idea of doing this chapter on chemical dependence and addiction is that there's just so much to say. It deserves much more attention than I can give here. That being said, since so many people are struggling (in what seems to be a crazier and crazier world), many are turning to substances or addictive behaviors to escape the madness. So please forgive my lack of depth as I address this important topic. I hope to provide some general information and direction so you can take steps forward.

What do you think of when you hear the word addiction? Most likely, you think of drug or alcohol addiction. However, even in my small practice, I work with those who are not only addicted to alcohol or drugs but others who are addicted to porn, shopping, eating and food, social media addiction (which we've addressed), cigarette and sex addiction. Of course, this is only a partial list. All are worthy topics to address. But for this book, I will discuss addiction more generally, emphasizing drugs and alcohol.

Are you addicted or dependent? Some use the words interchangeably. And some in the scientific community use neither word—they call it a "disorder" instead of addiction or dependence. Whatever term you use, it is not a moral failure.

Rather than getting lost in the differences, I will define addiction as an inability to stop using a substance or engaging in a behavior even though it is causing psychological, spiritual, or physical harm. So now, take a moment and ask yourself, what destructive activities or substances in your life are causing you or others distress? I say others because you may feel your use of substances or behavior isn't a problem. But what would others who are close to you say? You may have lost your objectivity. The good news is that this has been a chapter in your life. The story is not yet complete.

Drug and alcohol use in the United States costs $1.45 trillion in economic loss annually.[1] But more than the dollars lost, it is the loss of life and harm to individuals, families, and society that I find disturbing.

According to the CDC, roughly 850,000 Americans have died due to overdose since 1999. About three-quarters of these deaths involve oxycodone or heroin. Some of these deaths have been with prescribed opioids.[2]

With the legalization of marijuana, more and more people are using it. Although some say marijuana addiction isn't likely, psycholog-

[1] Drug and Alcohol Use in the United States Costs Over $1.45 Trillion Dollars Study by Recovery Centers of America Demonstrates
(PRNewsfoto/Recovery Centers of America)
NEWS PROVIDED BY
Recovery Centers of America
Mar 27, 2019, 08:18 ET

[2] Wide-ranging online data for epidemiologic research (WONDER). Atlanta, GA: CDC, National Center for Health Statistics; 2021.
Available at http://wonder.cdc.gov.
Mattson CL, Tanz LJ, Quinn K, Kariisa M, Patel P, Davis NL. Trends and Geographic Patterns in Drug and Synthetic Opioid Overdose Deaths — United States, 2013–2019. MMWR Morb Mortal Wkly Rep 2021;70:202–207. DOI: http://dx.doi.org/10.15585/mmwr.mm7006a4.

ical dependence can grow. Addiction or dependence? Again, in my mind, this is a difference with little distinction.

Marijuana has become increasingly potent. You can get hooked on marijuana. This means you can't stop using it, even if you want to. Maybe you say that it benefits you personally. Okay, but let me ask you, would you feel better on the morning of your major surgery if your doctor told you he just enjoyed a nice blunt? Or some great weed so that he'd be more relaxed? Probably not. Society depends on your sobriety.

In 2019, a person was killed every 52 minutes in a drunk driving crash in the United States.[3] Drunk drivers caused 40% of fatal car accidents.[4] The cost of addiction to society is enormous. It can lead to disease, theft, violence, and premature death. It destroys lives, families, and marriages. Whether or not you are "using", it costs us all.

Your addicted brain becomes numb, and your brain receptors become overwhelmed. The brain responds by producing less dopamine, the "feel-good hormone," or eliminating dopamine receptors. It's part of your brain's reward system, associated with pleasurable sensations, learning, memory, motor-system function, and more.

The cycle is this: you take your substance to feel good. It works for a while. Your brain produces less dopamine. Why? Because you just made it feel good artificially. It's doing its job of trying to find balance. Yet you still want to feel good. However, the everyday activities that pleased you before, like eating a good meal or laughing with friends, don't produce the same natural high because the brain produces less dopamine. So you use more to recapture the good feelings that seem harder to come by. And you use more. And more. But you feel less and less good naturally. So you use more. Addiction. You can't outrun your

[3] Yellman MA, Sauber-Schatz EK. Motor Vehicle Crash Deaths - United States and 28 Other High-Income Countries, 2015 and 2019. MMWR Morb Mortal Wkly Rep. 2022 Jul 1;71(26):837-843. doi: 10.15585/mmwr.mm7126a1. PMID: 35771709.

[4] Epidemiology and Consequences of Drinking and Driving Ralph Hingson, Sc.D., and Michael Winter, M.P.H.

brain's capacity to turn itself down—it's a race you're destined to lose from the start. Sobriety is the only way to win the race.

What are some of the signs or symptoms that indicate you may be suffering from addiction in general? An inability to stop the substance or destructive behavior and continuing despite the negative consequences; engaging in risky or unlawful behaviors; feeling preoccupied with the substance or behavior; seeing your relationships suffer; finding it increasingly difficult to follow through on commitments; and you don't enjoy what you used to.… these are just some of the signs of addiction.

There can be a genetic predisposition to substance abuse. The American Psychological Association (APA) states that "at least half of a person's susceptibility to drug or alcohol addiction can be linked to genetic factors."[5] (Sep 29, 2018) Therefore, if you have relatives who suffer from addiction, you can be forewarned and be more mindful.

Substance-related disorders impact the area of the brain responsible for emotions and decision-making. When addicted, your brain has been hijacked—your life has been stolen from you. But don't lose heart. Millions have been where you are and have found freedom from addiction. You are not alone.

Paul writes in Corinthians: "No trial has come to you but what is human. God is faithful and will not let you be tried beyond your strength; but with the trial he will also provide a way out, so that you may be able to bear it" (1 Corinthians 10:13). In other words, there is a way out of your addiction.

Addiction is nothing new. Moses spoke about drunkenness, orgies, and crazy, destructive behavior. By my rough count, Scripture mentions being drunk about 77 times. But of course, some of these times, Jesus was falsely accused of being a drunk. And on at least one occasion, we know he was quite the winemaker. But Scripture is squarely against drunkenness and addiction. Paul says, "… do not get

[5] https://www.apa.org/monitor/2008/06/genes-addict

drunk on wine, in which lies debauchery, but be filled with the Spirit …" (Ephesians 5:18).

To recover, you will first have to admit that you have a problem and that you'll need help. This is no easy admission, because you probably don't want to admit that a substance or behavior has control over you.

Although there are many treatment modalities for recovery, I'm a fan of The Fellowship of Alcoholics Anonymous and other 12-step programs. AA is for recovering alcoholics. However, there are many different 12-step programs based on AA's 12 steps, including those for narcotics, cocaine, overeaters, gamblers, etc.

AA is free. A big advantage. But more importantly, as a therapist, I've worked with many clients who have made great use of the program to stop using and transform their lives.

Recovery from addiction should not just be thought of as no longer abusing a substance. If, for example, you are an alcoholic but then locked in a cage with no access to alcohol, technically, you would no longer be abusing alcohol. But, in my opinion, you're still an alcoholic. You are not yet free from addiction. Recovery, whether from a substance or destructive activity, is more than just abstinence. It is about soul transformation. It is about relating to the world and self in a new way—it is about freedom from self *and* self-destruction. But to experience this life transformation, you must look in some dark places. What is the pain from which you're running?

AA recognizes that transformation should be a continual process for all. It isn't just about stopping drinking or drugging—although this is important. According to their literature, it is about "contented sobriety." It is a path of spiritual progress through a series of actions designed to elicit what *The Big Book of Alcoholics Anonymous* refers to as a "psychic change"[6]—a complete mental, emotional, and spiritual shift in attitudes and perception.

[6] Alcoholics Anonymous Big Book. 2002. 4th ed. New York, NY: Alcoholics Anonymous World Services.

For example, when clients see me because of anxiety or depression, I don't treat their anxiety or depression—I treat the person. I help them see how their perception of their life and memories of their experiences have shaped them. Our feelings are influenced by our perceptions, actions, and beliefs. Or, as they say in the program, you don't have a drinking or a drug problem—you have a thinking (self) problem. And the 12 Steps focus on fighting the battle of self. You quit fighting everything and everyone. Humility is the foundational principle in every step. You surrender to win, not fight. The 12 Steps lead to a spiritual awakening. They provide "relief from the bondage of self."

Another aspect I love about AA is the searching, fearless inventory of self (Step 4). Whether or not you're an addict, a humble reflection of your life is healthy. Another aspect, along with prayer, is making amends to those you've hurt. These are all restorative steps—these are godly steps.

Again, other successful programs are out there to help you address your addiction. You need to find what works for you. Chances are that you will fall or relapse along the way. The only requirement for membership is a desire to stop drinking, using, or engaging in destructive activity. Forgive yourself. The Fellowship is always welcoming. Live with the grace God offers. Get up and take another step—a small step.

Some psychologists say it takes about 21 days of conscious and consistent effort to create a new habit. However, changing your life will take far longer if you're addicted and abusing a substance or engaging in addictive behavior. But the rewards are beyond measure. The transformation from addiction to recovery is a journey—a lifetime journey. You need not hide. Work the steps. The desire will fade. Create a new lifestyle. Love yourself. Love others.

Next Steps ...

- First, pray for grace. You'll need it. Now, be honest with yourself. Is your life progressing? Are your relationships flourishing? Are you joyful or feel like you're just getting by? If you feel like you're no longer growing, how much time do you spend drinking, using, or thinking about drinking or using?

- Besides those you drink or use with, has anyone close to you suggested you may have a drinking or drugging problem? It may not be clear to you. If you're not sure, ask a trusted friend what they think. Or go to a therapist and discuss your use.

- If there are indications that you may be addicted, check out an AA meeting. They are everywhere, including online.

- Admitting that you have a problem takes courage. If you can do that, you've taken your first step toward recovery. It won't be easy. But others have been where you are. They want to help. You are not alone. Reach out for support. Pray. God is on your side.

9

MARRIAGE, MISERY, AND RESPONSIBILITY

G OD HATES DIVORCE (MALACHI 2:16). AND YOU PROBABLY do too. Especially if you've been through one or more. Divorce causes misery. So does a rotten marriage. But you don't have to choose to live in either the pain of divorce or the misery of your marriage. Interested in the alternative?

Some marriages should just never have happened. It's tough when you blow what is perhaps the most significant decision of your life. You might think you fall into that category—but maybe not.

And maybe you're in that group that's gotten married and divorced, and you're saying to yourself, "I understand the misery completely. I don't need to read more about it. And besides, I've found the 'perfect spouse!'" But wait! How do you know you're not making the same mistake?

According to some estimates, the divorce rate for first marriages is almost 50%; for second marriages, 60%;[1] and if you're really good at reading trends (but not particularly good at choosing spouses), you might be able to guess the rate of divorce for third marriages … Yup—70%. It seems you don't necessarily get better at this with experience.

Perhaps you're unmarried and wondering if you should skip this chapter. Don't. Why? Well, not just because you already paid for this chapter when you bought the book. But, more importantly, the

---

[1] According to some estimates, the divorce rate for first marriages is almost 50%; for second marriages, 60%from all of CDC.gov

information in this chapter can be applied to all your relationships! And you might still choose to marry—which could be awesome!

The U.S. Declaration of Independence states that the pursuit of happiness is protected as a fundamental human right with life and liberty. You have the right to pursue it, but how do you find it? The answer? The quality of your relationships will determine your happiness more than anything else. That's right. More than the perfect job; more than a mansion on a hill; more than winning the lottery, more than having the ideal body.

One of the most challenging yet rewarding client populations I work with is couples. It is rewarding because I know from research and experience that a happy marriage makes for a happy life, almost to the exclusion of everything else. Yes, you can have a healthy, loving marriage and still suffer from anxiety, depression, or other psychological maladies. But the relationship can greatly support healing with these other problems. So why is couples therapy so tricky? For several reasons. With individuals, you have one version of the story. Of course, the excellent therapist must use their imagination, fill in what is not being said or done by the other people not in the room but in their life, and challenge the client as to what is really going on. But it's generally not contentious. You listen to what the client is saying and offer support based on what they are telling you.

But with couples, you have two people in the room, usually with two very different versions of what is going on—it can get heated. During these times, I sometimes have to revert to my days of being a cop and take on a more active and controlling role.

"Stop. I hear what you're saying, but right now, I need to hear from your spouse," I say. One person generally doesn't like that, while the other smiles victoriously. Then the tables turn.

In cases where there is constant fighting and a volatile environment at home, studies show that it is healthier for children to be raised in a more peaceful, single-parent home.[2]

"What, Joe? Are you advocating divorce?"

No! I'm advocating for a healthy marriage. Ditch the volatility and discord, and strive for peace! But how do you get there?

People give many reasons why their marriage ended: finances, poor communication; differences over parenting; addiction, and infidelity. And these reasons are problematic. But there is one primary reason. And if you can fully appreciate the *one main* reason why divorce occurs, perhaps you can avoid it.

But, before I tell you why divorce occurs, I want to give you several reasons and motivations why you should fight for a healthy marriage. A few facts:

Researchers have found that marriage has a wide range of benefits, including improvements in individuals' economic well-being, mental and physical health, and the well-being of their children.

Those who are married tend to live longer, have fewer strokes and heart attacks, have a lower chance of becoming depressed, are less likely to have advanced cancer at the time of diagnosis, and are more likely to survive cancer[3] for a more extended period, and endure a major operation more often.

Studies have found that people in happy relationships have more robust immune function than those who are not.[4] Married people

[2] Marsh, S., Dobson, R. & Maddison, R. The relationship between household chaos and child, parent, and family outcomes: a systematic scoping review. BMC Public Health 20, 513 (2020). https://doi.org/10.1186/s12889-020-08587-8

[3] Social Relationships and Mortality Risk: A Meta-analytic Review
Julianne Holt-Lunstad , Timothy B. Smith , J. Bradley Layton
Published: July 27, 2010
https://doi.org/10.1371/journal.pmed.1000316

[4] Leschak CJ, Eisenberger NI. Two Distinct Immune Pathways Linking Social Relationships With Health: Inflammatory and Antiviral Processes. Psychosom Med. 2019 Oct;81(8):711-719. doi: 10.1097/PSY.0000000000000685. PMID: 31600173; PMCID: PMC7025456.

take fewer risks, eat better, and maintain healthier lifestyles. A healthy marriage supports better mental health. The married have lower rates of depression, loneliness, and social isolation, which have been associated with poorer health outcomes. Marriage is associated with shorter average hospital stays, fewer doctor visits, and reduced risk of nursing home admission. Married people and those in committed relationships are happier than single people. And if the dollars and cents matter, singles make less money than their married peers.[5]

And how does marriage affect your kids? Research shows that children raised by their married, biological parents tend to be healthier [6] (both mentally and physically) and do better in school than children not raised within marriage. Married parents are more likely to stay together than cohabiting ones. Two-thirds of cohabiting parents split up before their child reaches age 12, compared with one-quarter married parents.[7] There is a wealth of evidence that children raised by their biological, married parents have the best chance of becoming happy, healthy, and morally upright citizens in the future.[8] Mothers and fathers have unique and complementary roles in children's development. One study found that adults who perceived their

[5] Schoenborn, Charlotte A. "Marital Status and Health: United States, 1999-2002." Advance Data, no. 351, December 2004.

[6] Anderson J. The impact of family structure on the health of children: Effects of divorce. Linacre Q. 2014 Nov;81(4):378-87. doi: 10.1179/0024363914Z.000 00000087. PMID: 25473135; PMCID: PMC4240051.

[7] instability and child well-being." American Sociological Review 2007 72(2): 181-204; Craigie, T.L., J. Brooks-Gunn, and J. Waldfogel. "Family structure, family stability, and outcomes of five-year-old children." Families, Relationships, and Societies 2012 1(1): 43-61(19); Waldfogel J., T.A. Craigie, and J. Brooks-Gunn. "Fragile families and child wellbeing." The Future of Children 2010 20(2): 87-112.

2 Guzzo, K.B. and S.R. Hayford. "Fertility and the stability of cohabiting unions: Variation by intendedness." Journal of Family Issues 2014 35(4): 547-57

[8] Brown SL. Marriage and Child Well-Being: Research and Policy Perspectives. J Marriage Fam. 2010 Oct 1;72(5):1059-1077. doi: 10.1111/j.1741-3737.2010.00750.x. PMID: 21566730; PMCID: PMC3091824.

mothers as available and devoted to them in childhood were less likely to suffer from depression and low self-esteem [9] and more likely to be resilient in dealing with life events. Involved fathers produce children with better emotional health and attain higher job status as adults.[10] Married parents seem better able to offer more love and attention. This makes children less likely to engage in behaviors such as premarital sex, substance abuse, delinquency, and suicide. A healthy marriage provides a model for children's future marriage. Children of divorce have a shattered template for marriage, causing them to distrust marriage and avoid it for fear of divorce.[11] Studies have found that these children are twice as likely to cohabitate before marriage and divorce. Compared to children living with single parents, children conceived by married parents are safer; they are less likely to be aborted and are less likely to be abused or neglected. Children with married parents fare better economically. In the United States, poverty rates among children living with single mothers are five times higher than those of children living with married parents; a 2003 study of eleven industrialized countries found that children living in single-parent families have lower math and science scores than children in two-parent families. These are researched statistics, not my opinion.

I could go on and on, but I don't want you to get bored and start using this book as a paperweight, and I'm not writing a scientific journal. I simply want you to know that there is considerable science behind the value of marriage for you and your children.

[9] Umberson D, Pudrovska T, Reczek C. Parenthood, Childlessness, and Well-Being: A Life Course Perspective. J Marriage Fam. 2010 Jun;72(3):612-629. doi: 10.1111/j.1741-3737.2010.00721.x. PMID: 21869847; PMCID: PMC3159916

[10] Fisher SD. Paternal Mental Health: Why Is It Relevant? Am J Lifestyle Med. 2016 Feb 16;11(3):200-211. doi: 10.1177/1559827616629895. PMID: 30202331; PMCID: PMC6125083.

[11] Çetinkaya, Ş., & Erçin, E. (2015). The Psychological Problems Seen in the Children of Divorced Parents and the Nursing Approach Concerning These Problems. In (Ed.), Pediatric Nursing, Psychiatric and Surgical Issues. IntechOpen. https://doi.org/10.5772/59166

Now, back to my question. Why do marriages and relationships fail? Drum roll, please … d-i-s-t-a-n-c-e. Research shows that 80% of marriages break up because couples grow apart. They lose a sense of closeness and do not feel loved or appreciated.

I've never once heard a couple say to me, "we feel so bonded and close. The intimacy is just incredible. We just really like to fight." Or, "I feel great about myself and my spouse, and we love sharing our lives—but then I thought an affair might be a good idea."

We usually make *good and bad* decisions for understandable reasons. I'm not saying good reasons—but understandable.

When you lose that sense of closeness, all the other problems arise. I could write extensively about the issues that occur in marriage. But it would probably cause me to become depressed—and more importantly—it wouldn't be what is most beneficial for you. Instead, let's talk about solutions!

Many troubled marriages can be repaired. That might be hard to believe at times, but it's true. Research suggests that couples who can manage their conflict usually end up happier down the road than couples who divorce. Like faith in God, you may not see how things will work out; you don't have the answers, but you trust—that's faith. Trust. Even if you can't imagine having a loving marriage free of dysfunction, it doesn't mean it can't happen. Sometimes you have to hold on until you can begin making that journey toward one another again. And there are steps you'll have to take, but you've got first to give yourselves that opportunity.[12]

This does not mean that you're to tolerate abuse! I believe you have a moral obligation to do everything possible to keep yourself and your children safe. Domestic violence can cause lasting damage to yourself and your children if they witness the abuse. I've worked with hundreds

[12] Birditt KS, Brown E, Orbuch TL, McIlvane JM. Marital Conflict Behaviors and Implications for Divorce over 16 Years. J Marriage Fam. 2010 Oct;72(5):1188-1204. doi: 10.1111/j.1741-3737.2010.00758.x. PMID: 24058208; PMCID: PMC3777640.

of clients who, even as adults, still bear the scars of domestic violence in the home. But healing is possible.

If you're in an abusive relationship, get help now! Professional help. Some people can and want to provide support. If I were to write about domestic violence, it would take much more than a chapter. This chapter is about how to turn your marriage around and take those first steps toward each other.

If you're like most, it is probably easiest to see what your spouse is doing wrong. This doesn't make you a bad person. It's somewhat natural, and a problem that Jesus addressed:

"Why do you notice the splinter in your brother's eye but do not perceive the wooden beam in your own? How can you say to your brother, 'Brother, let me remove that splinter in your eye,' when you do not even notice the wooden beam in your eye? You hypocrite! Remove the wooden beam from your eye first; then you will see clearly to remove the splinter in your brother's eye" (Luke 6:41-42).

It requires great humility to look at your part. But it is necessary to stop the fight.

You will make no progress in moving toward one another while fighting. During an argument, you are not looking at solutions. You are not solving problems because your brain is not in creative mode. Your brain is in fight-or-flight mode. It is only interested in survival.

I've heard therapists speak and write about teaching couples how to "fight fair." In my opinion, this is an absurd notion. By definition, a fight is about winners and losers.

The late, great comedienne Phyllis Diller once wisely joked that the problem with winning a fight with your spouse means you have to go to bed with a loser.

If your goal is to restore your marriage, you must let go of the fight (hurting or killing the relationship) and flight (leaving the relationship either literally or emotionally). If you're still married but feel nothing, it may mean that you've checked out emotionally—you fled. This is understandable because feelings can become so overwhelming that you check out as a self-protective measure. You may believe this serves you, but you do not want to make this your lifelong position. Remember, your feelings are a part of what makes you human. Jesus felt so profoundly at His Passion that he sweat blood. But He didn't cut himself off from His feelings.

Positive feelings can return if you allow yourself to feel and take positive steps to restore the marriage. They will not return, however, if you focus exclusively on what is wrong in the union, wrong with your spouse, or even what is wrong with yourself. It only gives you fuel to fight. Remember, the goal is to restore the marriage, not to make your spouse a loser. So how do you stop the fighting?

Recognition of *your wrongdoing* is the first step. I've rarely seen couples continue to fight in my office if one says, "Hey, I'm sorry. I've made a mess of things. I see what I am doing as wrong...." This isn't simply an apology. And it doesn't fix the relationship. It is about taking responsibility for your actions.

Paul writes about criticism in Romans 2:1-2. "Therefore, you are without excuse, every one of you who passes judgment. For by the standard by which you judge another, you condemn yourself...."

Your critical spirit boomerangs. Ask yourself how you want to be treated. Now treat your spouse similarly. This doesn't mean you whitewash poor behavior, instead, it means you speak about it in a way oriented toward reconciliation.

This might mean you hold off on having tough conversations until you can do so without anger and criticism. This isn't avoidance—it's prudence. It's okay to wait until your anger has subsided to talk. I strongly recommend this. You both have a right to postpone talking about challenges until you can do so calmly. Yes. You might still be upset or disappointed, but anger is probably the biggest obstacle to resolving conflict effectively.

You can't change someone else, but you can change yourself. But you will not change anything about your behavior or thinking if you don't first take a beat and reflect on what *you're* doing.

Reflecting on your behavior isn't just about getting you to the point where you can say you're sorry. "Sorry" alone doesn't change behavior or solve problems, although asking for forgiveness is powerful. And when one does take responsibility for their actions, this is not the opportunity for the other to point out everything else they are doing wrong. Instead, use this as the opportunity for you to confess to *your wrongdoing*, contributing to the relationship's demise. Once you begin acknowledging your failures, the fighting stops, and you've now created the atmosphere in which to talk about solutions and work your way back toward one another.

Even in extreme cases where there has been an affair, there was probably a breakdown in the relationship that precipitated the infidelity. It's not about taking the blame or responsibility for someone else's wrong actions but allowing yourself to see your part.

Just as I wrote about guilt and shame, you don't want to continue beating yourself up about what you've done. Acknowledge your mistakes and take corrective steps.

Next Steps ...

- Ask yourself if you are withholding forgiveness. A clue that you may be is if you find yourself frequently angry or resentful with your spouse.

- Do you need to forgive yourself? A clue may be that your self-talk is harsh.

- Pray for your spouse. Bless them. Do small acts of kindness for them. As you begin to love them with your actions, notice the positive feelings within yourself.

- What can you substitute for fighting? Do you need to engage in more self-care? Get more exercise and more sleep?

- While not ignoring the problems, can you notice and comment on what is right with your spouse and marriage? Speak about it. It's easy to fall into negativity. Remind yourself and them why you chose to marry them.

10

MARRIAGE, FORGIVENESS, AND RECONCILIATION

YOU MAY CONFUSE SAYING SORRY WITH FORGIVENESS and forgiveness with reconciliation.

I've heard clients say, "I said I was sorry. What else does he want?" And, "She said she forgave me. So why can't we be together again?" Also, "I'm not going to forgive until they say they are sorry and ask for forgiveness."

It can be confusing. So let's set the record straight, shall we?

God says you must forgive. A command. Period. You m-u-s-t forgive. Look no further than the Lord's Prayer found in Matthew 6. "… Forgive us our trespasses (or sins) as we forgive others…."

God forgave you and reconciled you. And you, too, must forgive. However, reconciliation is something different….

Scripture doesn't say someone has to ask for forgiveness in order for you to forgive. They don't have to say I'm sorry. It doesn't depend on them making up for their misdeeds.

Forgive.

"What? But what they did is so terrible! I can't forgive," you say.

Yes. You must. Trust me.

You want to forgive not only because God says you must, but for your sake, you must forgive. Understandably, you may withhold forgiveness because you don't understand what it implies and the ramifications on your well-being.

You must forgive. Scripture does not say, however, that you must reconcile. If your marriage is on the rocks, and you want to stay married (and I hope you do), then yes, you must reconcile. Reconciliation is more than forgiveness.

But let's say you have a friend who has hurt you. Must you forgive? Yes. Must you reconcile? No. Although you may want to. And the following principles will apply to all your relationships.

In the previous chapter, I gave compelling reasons for you to create a healthy and vibrant marriage: you, your kids, and society benefit. But you must first understand the difference between forgiveness and reconciliation.

Forgiveness is the greatest gift you can give *yourself*. Stop thinking you are doing someone a huge favor by saying, "I forgive you." It might be a wonderful gift to give to someone else, but believe it or not, you are the first and probably the greatest beneficiary of forgiveness.

When you choose to forgive, you will not pay back what someone did to you. It implies no retaliation. It means you let go of your anger, hurt, and resentment.

It's wonderfully freeing to know that you don't need anyone else's cooperation to forgive. You don't need to wait for someone to say they are sorry before you can forgive. What if they never apologize? Perhaps they've died, moved away, or are no longer part of your life? Are you going to hold on to the anger and resentment? You would not be punishing them by withholding forgiveness but only punishing yourself.

Remember in the Gospel of Matthew, chapter 18. Peter asked Jesus how many times he had to forgive. "Seven times?" Peter asked.

"No. Seven times seventy times," Jesus replied. And for you wise guys, he didn't mean 490 times. He meant an infinite number of times.

However many times you've been hurt is the number of times you must forgive. When you experience the true freedom of forgiveness, you will be far less interested in the fight and withholding forgiveness—you will be setting yourself free.

Research has shown that the act of forgiveness has significant rewards and positively impacts your health. It reduces the risk of heart attack, improves cholesterol levels and sleep, reduces pain and blood pressure, and reduces feelings of anxiety, depression, and stress.[1]

Why do you experience these many health benefits when you forgive? It comes down to the brain-body connection, and again, fight-or-flight. Let me explain.

The brain, I like to say, is wonderfully gullible. It is open to believing what you tell it. And the brain, in turn, tells the body how to respond. For instance, if you go to a scary movie, which I don't recommend, you become afraid. That is, after all, the goal of those who make scary films. But the fear doesn't just remain in your brain. Your body responds as though what is happening on the screen is really happening. Your blood pressure increases, your heart races, your palms sweat, etc. These are just a few of the reasons I avoid scary movies.

When you withhold forgiveness, it means you still have a focus on how you were hurt. And, in turn, how you intend to punish the offender. In other words, you are maintaining the fight or remembering that you must flee. And your body responds when you are in fight-or-flight mode. It remains hyper-vigilant. The blood pressure stays higher—your body holds onto fat if it needs the energy. This compromises your immune system because your body isn't focusing on healing as it does during rest periods. I could go on and on.

When you forgive, your body also responds, but in a positive way. When you forgive, you let go of the anger, resentment, and ideas of retaliation. You let go of the fight.

But don't think you haven't forgiven just because you hold complicated feelings or thoughts. Forgiveness is a choice to move differently. You don't necessarily feel different when you forgive. It's possible. But you may have complex feelings and doubts about the relationship for a good reason—you've been hurt. You're not sure how reconciliation can or should take place. But you can figure that out with time, work, and help.

[1] Weir, K. (2017, January 1). Forgiveness can improve mental and physical health. Monitor on Psychology, 48(1). https://www.apa.org/monitor/2017/01/ce-corner

You may be withholding forgiveness because you mistakenly believe that to forgive means you are giving the wrongdoer a "pass," that what they did is okay, or that their behavior is excusable. This is not true. Forgiveness doesn't mean you forget or dismiss someone else's bad behavior. When you forgive, you are first taking care of yourself. You are allowing your body, soul, and brain to heal. Forgive for *your* sake.

In the story of the Prodigal Son told in the Gospel of Luke, chapter 15, much attention is given to the son who tells his father he's dead to him (kind of like a Godfather movie moment) by asking for his inheritance now. The son then leaves the family and lives a life of debauchery. When the son acknowledges that he's made a mess of his life, not to mention he's broke, he decides to return to his father. He realizes he has sinned greatly and admits as much.

This, of course, is a beautiful lesson for us. We need to humble ourselves rather than make excuses for our actions. Again, as mentioned above, accepting responsibility for what we've done wrong would eliminate much fighting. The son represents all of us, and his humility is the example for us to follow. God is always there to welcome you back. You are never beyond His love.

But the father also provides the best example of how you are to forgive. Yes, the father in this story represents God and expresses his unconditional love and forgiveness as we turn toward him. But I contend that it also gives us the perfect model for how we are to forgive others when they have sinned against us.

The father doesn't hold onto a grudge when the son leaves. He isn't angry. He isn't plotting revenge. Before the son even gets back to the house, the father, we are told, is watching for his return. He races out to meet the son with enthusiasm. He doesn't allow the son to grovel. He throws his arms around him, lavishes him with gifts, then throws a party to end all parties! What set the stage for the party, for reconciliation? The father's attitude of forgiveness.

When you forgive immediately, your mood will be lighter. You will be in a position to move forward.

Now that you've forgiven, you can take that next step to reconcile, if appropriate. Remember, reconciliation is about bringing the relationship back with changes. You wouldn't want a return to "normal" if normal were dysfunctional.

If, for instance, your spouse abuses you somehow, you can forgive, but you can't reconcile the relationship without significant changes. Simply, no more abuse. It should not be tolerated. Period.

In this case, it is probably necessary for both parties to get professional help. The abuser needs to understand why he abuses and, more importantly, how to act without violence. The abused must understand how the abuse hurt them and how to heal. You can't ignore the abuse, even if you forgive.

Remember the woman caught in the act of adultery? (John 8) Jesus offered forgiveness, but he also said, don't sin anymore. He called for a behavior change.

Whatever the hurt, reconciliation includes forgiveness but is more. It means creating a new relationship but with the same person.

In Luke 10, Jesus instructs his disciples to go out and share the Gospel, offering forgiveness and reconciliation with God, which would ultimately come from His sacrifice on the cross. (For an excellent book on this topic, I suggest Fr. Dave Heney's book, *Luke 10 Leadership - How to Succeed at Parish Ministry*.) But if the Message is rejected, He tells His disciples they are to wipe the dust from their feet and move on. They are not to take offense or retaliate. Forgiveness but no reconciliation.

Keep in mind, however, that Jesus is referring to strangers here. If a family member or spouse rejects you, you can't simply walk away. The relationship carries weight and, hopefully, permanence. Thus the need for reconciliation. So what would this look like?

An excellent model for reconciliation can be found in what Catholics call the Sacrament of Reconciliation. It is not called the Sacrament of Forgiveness. Why? Because although forgiveness is undoubtedly part of it, it is about reconciling or creating a relationship anew.

The four steps of Reconciliation are Contrition, Confession, Penance, and Absolution. As I am a therapist and not a priest, let's look at what it could look like in a relationship, not the confessional. For our purposes here, let's use one particular "sin": yelling at your spouse, and apply this four-step model ...

One: Contrition. A contrite heart feels sorrow and remorse for having hurt the other person. It is an appropriate expression of guilt. Remember our earlier chapter on guilt? Guilt is a force for good if your pain leads you to correct your behavior. You've yelled at your spouse. Perhaps this caused them to feel fear or belittled, or disrespected. You feel bad for having hurt them. You allow yourself to feel their pain. This is called empathy— which directs you to the next step ...

Two: Confession. You confess or acknowledge what you've done to your spouse. Although motivation or understanding the reasons behind what you've done can be challenging, this can also provide an opportunity for meaningful dialogue. It's more than just saying sorry or saying what you've done. It's a profound search to understand why you've yelled, how it hurts, and what needs to change so that you can reconcile. It could also include planning how to avoid any future yelling. Additionally, another critical consideration as you explore the "why" in "what" happened, you may have prejudged what you see as "sin" or harmful behavior. In the example we are using for this exercise, yelling, it is clear what is being done and how it may be hurtful. However, you may be prejudging an event before fully knowing the circumstances. For example, let's say your husband is late returning from work. You get angry and blast him for being inconsiderate upon his return. Then he explains that an accident occurred right in front of him and he was nearly involved. He stopped to render aid. This may seem like an extreme example, but there are times when the harm caused was unintentional or a misunderstanding. If you jump to conclusions before having a meaningful dialogue, you are more likely to fight and cause yourself distress. There may have been no intention of causing harm or hurt. Pause. Don't assume the worst. Your premature response will not help you.

Three: Penance is an outward act to repair what was done. Remember, God commands you to love. Love isn't just refraining from hurting someone. It is a commitment to act charitably. It's prosocial behavior. Your penitential acts, in this case, aren't just refraining from yelling but speaking tenderly and lovingly.

Four: Absolution. This is living out the reconciled and amended relationship. It is a relationship made afresh. It includes all of the above steps. It is your relationship restored, healed, and whole—it is living love.

Of course, as imperfect beings, you will always make mistakes. And just as God offers you His grace, so must you have grace for the relationship and your spouse. Grace allows for errors. It doesn't hold others to unreasonable, impossible standards. Again, in the story of the woman caught in adultery, Jesus pointed out that all others have also sinned. Throw the stone if you are sinless, Jesus told them. None did.

Too often, when we've been hurt or things aren't going well, we focus on what is wrong. Again, understandable. But more importantly, we must get clarity on *what we want to happen*. Rather than just saying what hurt you (past tense) can you frame what you do want (future tense)? Even if you wanted to, living in the past is impossible. You can, however, chart a course for a better future. So, what might this look like? Here is a simple example.

Let's say you get bugged when your husband doesn't call you when he's running late. You could say, "It's insulting that you don't call me! You don't care about my feelings."

Now how would you respond to this attack? Would you say, "You're right. I am rude and uncaring." Probably not. It's more likely that you would defend yourself in some way, including a counterattack. The fight is on, and reconciliation is unlikely.

However, using this same example, if you said with sincerity and tenderness, "Honey, I love you, and I worry when you don't come home on time. I want to spend more time with you." In all likelihood, this will be met with a far more loving response and result in a behavior change—reconciliation.

Frequently, when couples come to me, they say they don't communicate well. But what does this mean?

It usually means that they fight. A lot. Attack. Defend. Counterattack. I've never seen this strategy lead to reconciliation. Of course, you probably don't want to fight but are unsure how to break this vicious cycle. So how do you do that?

Good communication prioritizes listening and understanding. And this requires cooperation. Some therapists advocate this approach and think it can happen with a simple use of "I statements" and a concentration on feelings. I don't support this approach. Why?

Using this approach, you could say to your spouse, "I feel miserable, and it's all your fault. You're a jerk." Technically, you're using the requisite "I statements" and speaking honestly about your feelings.

But how would you respond if your spouse said this to you? Probably not well, because it still includes an attack. Your feelings are valid, and you're certainly right to have and express them, but *how you do it* matters most. If, instead, you said something like, "I'm miserable. I don't feel like this relationship is working as it is. I want to do my part to improve it. I want our marriage to survive. Perhaps if *we* …"

In this example, you're still using "I statements" and sharing your feelings. But what you're doing here is talking about what *you want* with a focus on solutions. Using "we" also shows that you are accountable for bringing about change as a couple. It's less threatening than pointing fingers at your spouse, demanding that they make all the changes.

While one speaks, the other listens without interruption, then shows that they understand with words *and attitude.* So, the response begins with acknowledging what the other said and wants. You cannot simply parrot what the other said. The response must show understanding. After you've demonstrated that you understand your partner, you can speak from your perspective. Drop the attack, and take responsibility for what you've done and what you can do differently. Now you are having a conversation that can lead to reconciliation.

You want to feel loved and appreciated. It's what makes you feel like you matter. But you must first understand what makes you feel this way. It would help if you then expressed it positively. Believe it or not, this can be difficult. For one reason, when things aren't going well, we tend to get a clear picture of what we don't want and what makes us feel rotten. It sometimes takes extra effort to turn this around and remember what it is that we *do* want. What makes you feel loved and appreciated?

One exercise I like to have couples do is the "I Feel Loved When You ..." exercise. (Okay. Probably not the catchiest title, but it's effective.) So what would this look like?

Sitting near each other, turn to your spouse and say, "I feel loved when you ..." Now fill in the blank. It might be as simple as, "I feel loved when you bring me coffee." Then your spouse might say, "I feel loved when you give me an unexpected hug." You go back and forth. State this in a positive way. It's not as helpful to say, "I don't feel loved when you come home late." Instead, say, "I feel loved when you spend time with me."

This may be a challenging exercise for several reasons. But let me focus on the primary reason this is difficult. You may never have developed the skill to express what you want, what makes you feel loved. Why? Perhaps when you were a child, you tried to communicate your wants and were shot down in such a way that you learned you weren't entitled to have wants and needs.

Let's say the six-year-old-you goes to your father and says, "Daddy, I really want to go to Disneyland ! Can we go?" And your dad abruptly erupts, "No! We cannot go to Disney! You know we can't afford that!" At six, of course, you can't grasp what the family can or cannot afford.

But one thing you've learned for sure: it's not safe or okay to express what you want. Perhaps now, as an adult, you're not even sure what you want. You've shut down that part of your life. You don't deserve to have wants, you think to yourself. Then it's no surprise that you feel like your needs don't matter. You don't know what you want, so you can't express what you want.

Remember, it wasn't the one big thing that made you fall in or out of love. It was the many little things. As you focus on expressing your wants and giving to each other, focus on the little things. Even if you won the lottery, you'd return to your previous level of happiness after about one year. If you're fortunate, that would be a once-in-a-lifetime event. But the small acts of kindness, the demonstrations of appreciation, can make a lifetime of bliss. Mother Teresa famously said, "We can do no great things, only small things with great love."

You must understand what you want for your life and your marriage. But now let me tell you something you may find hard to believe: happily married couples report getting their wants met s-e-l-d-o-m. That's right. This is not a typo. You don't always need to get what you want from your spouse. Getting what you want does not make you happy or your marriage thrive. You are not entitled to get everything you want. But you are entitled to your wants being respected. What does this look like?

Let's say you want to go to dinner with your husband on Saturday night, so you tell him. But then he reminds you, saying, "Honey, I'd love to spend time with you, but remember I invited your mom to spend the weekend and promised her to have a big family meal on Saturday evening?"

In this case, he is showing respect for your wants. You're still not getting what you want, but when we acknowledge wants, we remind people that they matter.

God wants you to pray about everything. But you don't have to be a theologian to know that just because you ask God, He will give you everything you want.

By nature, children are "want machines." But a good parent knows you can't give them everything they want. It's sometimes not doable or a good idea. That's why you generally eat your vegetables before the chocolate cake. (Not always in my house. But usually.) And you don't want to quash your children's enthusiasm and spirit. So, you do what is best for them without giving in to their desires.

Similarly, you don't want to quash your spouse's desires and enthusiasm. Share the excitement of the want, even when you can't give them what they want. After all, what you both want and need the most is connection. Show that respect for their desires.

Happy marriages are based on friendship, respect, and enjoyment of each other. Your feelings can change because of weather, hunger, traffic, bad news, lack of sleep, etc. But you can choose how to treat each other, no matter how you feel. And when you treat each other well, it is more likely that your feelings about the relationship will improve.

Even your memory of events will be biased depending on your mood. Memory can be a tricky and unreliable thing. If you are in a bad mood, you will be more likely to remember your past negatively and vice versa. But successful couples work to remember the past with fondness. If you distort history negatively, you will likely project a doubtful future.

If you struggled financially in the beginning, or your Uncle Joe fell into the wedding cake (I didn't. It was someone else.), you can laugh about it and marvel at how you overcame such adversity, or you can grumble that it was only a portend of life to come.

Love isn't a feeling. It is a choice. You may have gotten married for one particular reason, whatever it was. You may choose to stay married and create a vibrant marriage now for another [reason]. Choose wisely. See what is best in each other

Next Steps ...

- Ask yourself what you want. Do you want a vibrant, loving marriage? Create an image of what that is and speak about it.

- Reflect on your behavior. Without beating yourself up, take stock of what you've done poorly, and more importantly, commit to making small, positive steps.

- Even if you don't feel loving, treat your spouse kindly. Show your love with small acts of kindness and sacrifice. Treat them as you would a good friend. Be specific and commit to three small, kind actions a day.

- See what is good in your spouse. Focus on that. Tell them. Let them know. Until it becomes automatic, engage in the Love and Appreciation exercise. This could be a daily exercise.

- If there are struggles you need to speak about, make a mutually-agreed upon date to do so when you are not angry. If the conversation becomes heated, take a break. Make another date to return to the discussion.

- Remember, it is easy to see what is wrong with the relation-ship. Speak about what you are doing when the relationship is going well. Keep in mind that your children are watching. You will be modeling the behavior they will expect and act out in their future relationships!

- Marriage will provide you with many opportunities to practice reconciliation. Use the above-mentioned Contrition, Confession, Penance, and Absolution model to bring about the amended relationship. You have been treated gracefully by God. Treat each other with the same grace that has been extended to you.

11

RESILIENCE

A S I MENTIONED BEFORE, I RUN. I HATE RUNNING. IT'S A stupid sport. At least, that's what I tell myself while I'm doing it. Then I recover after a brutal run and say something like, "That was awesome!" And after a few days, I get excited to go for a run again.

It's probably a stretch to say running is the perfect metaphor for life. But I do think it offers some important lessons.

You make a plan to do something big and vital. That's the "I'm excited to go for a run" part. You put on your shoes and shorts, and you hydrate. That's the "preparation to do something important" part. Then you go running—that's the important thing. But it might also be the thing that causes you much pain. And if, in your pain, you still recognize that what you're doing is essential—and that you need to get back up or keep going—what do you do?

You might hit your first wall very early on in your essential venture. It takes me a couple of hundred yards to remember how much I hate running. But I push on. Now you might think, "Wow, Joe. How do you push on after 200 whole yards? Incredible!" And to think I've been doing this for decades....

You might look at some people—whether great athletes or successful in business—and say, "They just got it."

No. They don't just "got it." But they may have developed "it." And so can you!

Resilience is not a fixed trait. You don't either have it or not. It is a learned trait. *You* can learn it. And why should you?

Whatever you choose to do with your life, whether it's to grow in holiness, improve your relationships, go to college, or raise kids, you will benefit from becoming more resilient.

You must begin by understanding that God created you for a *lifetime* of change and growth. Scripture and science both support this notion. And to experience continuous growth, you must be resilient. You might think, "that ship has sailed", that it's too late for you. Not true.

Abraham, who God said would become the father of many nations, first heard of this plan when he was about ninety years old. He was about one hundred years old when his wife Sarah finally gave birth to their first son. Sarah, the younger woman, was about ninety. And you think today's kids are waiting a long time to start their families!

Your brain can create new neural pathways throughout your life. This means you can continue learning, developing new skills, and growing intellectually. Wherever you see yourself today, you are not stuck. Your life can continue to evolve. Science has only more recently come to understand this phenomenon. Scripture, however, has recognized this from the beginning. Literally and figuratively, you can teach an old dog new tricks!

Why, just a couple of months ago, I took on the challenge of teaching my faithful dog, Riley, how to shake. She is well into her middle years. I now refer to her as "Riley the Princess Circus Dog who can Ambi-Shake." A long name, but well deserved. She follows me around all day, high-fiving me with both paws—to the point of irritation. I may just teach her how to go back to taking long naps. But enough about my dog, let's get back to you!

In the psych biz, we recognize the difference between a growth mindset and a fixed mindset. It's pretty much what it sounds like. You can either grow and develop new skills, or believe you're stuck with what you've got and where you are. You may *feel* stuck, which is understandable. But you are not.

Allow me to provide you with another example of the growth mindset from Scripture: "As [Jesus] was walking by the Sea of Galilee, he saw two brothers, Simon, who is called Peter, and his brother Andrew, casting a net into the sea; they were fishermen. He said to them, 'Come after me, and I will make you fishers of men'. At once, they left their nets and followed him" (Matt. 4:18-20). They caught fish for a living. They were well-established and probably well into their middle age. Yet, they responded to God and slowly developed into preachers and evangelists who we still read today. Your life can be radically different, filled with purpose and meaning—with God calling you. You can continue to develop a more vibrant life.

You may have reasons why you think your life can't be different, improved, and experience growth. But you can either listen to the fear in your head and heart or listen to God and begin a new, exciting journey.

Let me provide one more example from Scripture: God called Moses to lead His people out of slavery. Moses had some good excuses as to why he shouldn't be the one to do it. Listen to this:

"On one occasion, after Moses had grown up, when he had gone out to his relatives and witnessed their forced labor, he saw an Egyptian striking a Hebrew, one of his relatives. Looking about and seeing no one, he struck down the Egyptian and hid him in the sand. The next day he went out again, and now two Hebrews were fighting! So he asked the culprit, 'Why are you striking your companion?' But he replied, 'Who has appointed you ruler and judge over us? Are you thinking of killing me as you killed the Egyptian?' Then Moses became afraid and thought, 'The affair must certainly be known.' When Pharaoh heard of the affair, he sought to kill Moses. But Moses fled from Pharaoh and went to the land of Midian." (Exodus 2:11-22).

But murder and fear wasn't Moses's only excuse. He also pointed out to God that he wasn't good with words and stuttered. He doesn't sound like the perfect person to lead, does he? God thought otherwise.

Moses had to overcome other tremendous obstacles as he led God's people out of slavery. He had to fight battles against superior forces—sometimes against giants! The people frequently complained to him about the harsh conditions in which they lived. Life was so bad that, at one time, they wanted to return to slavery in Egypt versus moving toward freedom in the Promised Land. Moses instructed the people in the ways of the one true God: *Yahweh*, but the people sometimes abandoned their faith to follow gods who promoted child sacrifice and orgies, etc. Indeed, Moses had plenty of reason to question his ability to teach and lead, but he persevered and prevailed—he grew. And so can you when you develop the faith and the right mindset!

To develop *resilience*, the capacity to get back on your feet and keep moving when life is challenging, you must first challenge what you consider failure. I'd ask that you replace the word "failure" with "setback." Failure is an "all-is-lost" word, whereas "setback" is temporary. A setback is an opportunity to learn. There is no growth without resistance and setbacks. You can train to get back up when you expect to get knocked down.

Some recent research has shown that it isn't beneficial to praise natural talent and ability but rather to reward persistence and resilience.[1] Those that believe in the growth mindset and resilience are less prone to depression.[2] Why? Feeling stuck and thinking, "I've failed," can lead to depression. But when you recognize setbacks are to be expected, you can grow, not despite the setback, but *because* of the setback—that can be pretty exciting! Recognize and celebrate growth.

Although it might be natural to stay where you feel comfortable and safe, this is not where you grow and develop resilience. God speaks about this in the parable of the talents found in the Gospel of Matthew, chapter 25. The Master (God) gave out various skills (or talents) to his workers. He then went away. And when He returned, He

---

[1] The Secret to Raising Smart Kids
HINT: Don't tell your kids that they are. More than three decades of research shows that a focus on "process"—not on intelligence or ability—is key to success in school and in life /By Carol S. Dweck on January 1, 2015

[2] Tao W, Zhao D, Yue H, Horton I, Tian X, Xu Z, Sun HJ. The Influence of Growth Mindset on the Mental Health and Life Events of College Students. Front Psychol. 2022 Apr 14;13:821206. doi: 10.3389/fpsyg.2022.821206. PMID: 35496212; PMCID: PMC9046553.

asked the workers what they had done with the talents. Those who had risked and increased what they had been given were rewarded. But one failed to do anything. He saw that he was given little and chose to do nothing with what he was given. Fear immobilized him. He was called wicked and punished for his inaction.

You have been given talents. You will discover your purpose and meaning in life when you take what God has given you and grow it. Near the end of your life, it is doubtful that you will celebrate a safe life. But if you can reflect on how you risked, how you got back onto your feet when knocked down, and how you did more than you thought possible, that will be a well-lived life.

"Therefore, since we are surrounded by so great a cloud of witnesses, let us rid ourselves of every burden and sin that clings to us and persevere in running the race that lies before us while keeping our eyes fixed on Jesus, the leader and perfecter of faith...." (Hebrews 12:1-2).

Run. Fall. Get back up, then run to win!

Next Steps ...

- What do you say to yourself when life is difficult? What belief mindset, and voice would give you more energy to get back up?

- What would you do differently if you knew God might ask you to risk? Remember, He has called you to a lifetime of growth.

- What is one stretch activity you can do today to take you out of your comfort zone?

- Rather than seeing your limitations, what areas in your life that can be grown? Take small steps and focus on the journey, not the destination.

12

HAPPINESS, JOY,
AND THE CROSS

WHAT DO YOU CARE ABOUT? WHAT ARE THE THINGS (you do or acquire) that make you happy? Do these activities or things bring you joy? Is there a difference between happiness and joyfulness? Can you experience joy while carrying your cross as God asks you to? And have you ever started a book chapter with so many questions?

I love the beach, waterskiing, and snow skiing. I love a cold beer with friends and a warm steak right off the barbecue. I love to play hard. But these aren't the things I'm passionate about—they simply make me happy.

You might love watching football with friends on a Sunday, chocolate cake, or shopping—these are pleasures. They probably even make you happy, but does the happiness last?

I want to invite you to consider your pursuit of happiness and suggest you pursue a life of joy instead. The same God that says He wants you to experience joy, but not necessarily happiness, also asks you to pick up your cross and follow Him—sounds like a contradiction, but maybe not. I'll explain.

At the end of your life, you may have done many things that made you happy (or at least you thought they would make you happy), but you still might say that your life was meaningless. Why? No joy. And no joy because there is no cross. Momentarily, I will present perhaps the world's best example of this. But first, I want to make an essential distinction between joy and happiness as I understand it. You may think of the two as interchangeable—many do.

Happiness has many definitions. Generally, it is often described as involving positive emotions and feelings—it *feels* good—so we pursue it.

Ironically, however, doing those things and having those things you think will make you happy sometimes do not, particularly in the long run. You've probably experienced this yourself. You get that new car and are super excited—you're happy. But the months wear on, and you've been making those car payments, the increased insurance payments, and soon that car that made you so happy becomes simply transportation—and it's more challenging to be excited about transportation. Even if you think about the day you bought the car, it probably doesn't bring you happiness. However, let's say that the same number of months go by that you purchased the vehicle, but instead, you invested in someone else's life. Perhaps you gave to a charity and lifted a family out of poverty. Now when you think back on that day of your generosity, realizing that you did something significant for someone else, you are more likely to remember that day fondly and more profoundly: That, is joy.

Let me return momentarily to one of my silly examples of things that make me happy: Steak. I've had more than a few in my lifetime. However, no matter how hard I try, I just can't muster up happy feelings when I think about the one I consumed a few weeks back. There was one, however, I recall joyfully. A couple of years ago, friends took my wife and me to a great restaurant, and they insisted I order the expensive steak. I didn't want to disappoint them. And as I recall, it was terrific! The waiter insisted the cow died stress-free because she—the cow—listened to smooth jazz before her unsuspecting demise. That was one of the semi-secret keys to their great-tasting meat. As I reflect on that wonderful night, I reminisce about the love and laughter shared with our dear friends. We wondered if the cow preferred Kenny G or the more traditional Art Pepper. The steak made me happy at the moment, but the joy I experienced, as I recall that night, reflects the more profound connection with our dear friends. Sorry, jazz-loving cow.

Winning the lottery will likely make you happy, at least for a while. If winning the lottery takes you out of the stress of poverty, it can give you a sense of greater life *satisfaction*, which can last for a long while; after all, the stress of poverty is real. But for the most part, the level of *happiness* seems to return to where it was before the financial windfall for folks lucky enough to win.

Conversely, adverse life circumstances, even extreme ones like a severe car accident, the loss of a loved one, etc., are likely to make you sad or depressed for a while. Then eventually, probably sooner than you think, and unexpectedly, you will return to your level of happiness before you experienced the tremendous setback. Of course, this doesn't preclude the possibility of experiencing post-traumatic stress or depression after trauma. But with the proper support, you can experience how wonderfully resilient God made you!

Now I could bore you with scores of studies and anecdotal evidence that support the above assertions, but I think by now you know that I'm not into boring—and probably neither are you. So why doesn't pursuing and acquiring the things you think will make you happy keep you happy? The psychobabble term for this is called hedonic adaptation. You return to your "set point" of happiness after experiencing the highs and lows. If, for example, your favorite thing in the world is to go to Disneyland, and you go 100 days in a row, you will not experience the same incredible excitement or happiness as you did on day one of your visit to the Magic Kingdom. So, one of the tricks to keeping extraordinary adventures or activities fun is to allow yourself to experience them rarely—chasing happiness doesn't work.

However, there is a lovely alternative: to embrace the cross and allow your life to be transformed and filled with joy that doesn't fluctuate like happiness. Joy is more profound and far less dependent on your circumstances or on getting everything you think will make you happy. It is about connecting your life with meaning and purpose. Giving. Joy is being grateful for your blessings and loving and connecting with others. Sacrifice. And yes, the cross.

As promised, the world's most noteworthy example demonstrates that "having" and "getting" don't equate to joy or happiness....

King Solomon, David's son, was hailed as the wisest of men during his lifetime. People from all over the world would consult him about nearly everything: building, trading, plants, making money, and settling family disputes … he amassed a massive fortune that amounted to tons and tons of gold and silver. Scripture reports he had 700 wives and 300 concubines. (Good luck keeping them all happy!) He undertook colossal building projects, including homes, aqueducts, and gardens, and his crowning achievement was to build a grand temple for worshiping God. He did it all. He had it all. His pursuit of pleasure was unsurpassed! Yet, at the end of his own life, he confessed he hated life. He was miserable. His words: "But when I turned to all the works that my hands had wrought, and to the fruit of the toil for which I had toiled so much, see! all was vanity and a chase after wind. There is no profit under the sun" (Ecclesiastes 2:11). This, I say, epitomizes the empty pursuit of happiness.

Trauma won't make you happy, but what you do after the traumatic event may make you joyful! Yes. Trauma may initially leave you feeling shocked, confused, betrayed, and lost—but it doesn't have to end there unless you allow it.

You are probably familiar with the term Post-traumatic Stress. Post-traumatic Stress Disorder (PTSD) is an affliction that develops in some people who have experienced a shocking, scary, or dangerous event. It is natural to feel afraid during *and after* a traumatic situation. Fear triggers the body to help defend against danger or to avoid it. But for those who have PTSD, the triggering, anxiety, and fear can stay long after the traumatic event. It is treatable, but while it remains, it can be unbearable for some. But the other term you may be less familiar with is Post-Traumatic Growth.

Post-Traumatic Growth is a life that becomes deeper with meaning and joy after the traumatic event. It begins by recognizing that you can move beyond being a victim. You may not initially believe you have what it takes to recover—this is understandable. But I want to remind you that with God on your side, who or what can stand against you? Post-traumatic Growth doesn't mean you forget what happened to you; it means that you've learned to live more deeply. You develop stronger relationships, greater awareness of new possibilities, increased personal strength, spiritual enhancement, and a deeper appreciation for life.

Let me again offer an example from Scripture in my biblical hero, Paul. He liked to brag about his calamities, his trauma. Not because he wanted to lay hold of victimhood, but because it glorified God to show how he was able to overcome with God working through him. I like to call it Paul's resume:

"[I've had] far greater labors, far more imprisonments, far worse beatings, and numerous brushes with death. Five times at the hands of the Jews I received forty lashes minus one. Three times I was beaten with rods, once I was stoned, three times I was shipwrecked, I passed a night and a day on the deep; on frequent journeys, in dangers from rivers, dangers from robbers, dangers from my own race, dangers from Gentiles, dangers in the city, dangers in the wilderness, dangers at sea, dangers among false brothers; in toil and hardship, through many sleepless nights, through hunger and thirst, through frequent fastings, through cold and exposure" (2 Corinthians 11: 23-29).

You may have experienced trauma, but let's go ahead and admit that this ranks in the top ten of a tough life lived. Yet Paul, as opposed to Solomon, lived a life of joy, purpose, and meaning. Paul came to understand that his weakness and trials made him stronger. Why? Because with less of him, there was more of God. His sacrifices were for others. As his reliance on God became increasingly apparent, so too did his sense of purpose, meaning, and joy grow.

Joy isn't a result of what happens to you but how you respond to your life circumstances, including the blessings you experience. You can live with overflowing abundance, but if you fail to recognize it with gratitude, you will experience neither happiness nor joy. Again, happiness is more ephemeral and depends on life going your way. But Paul's life demonstrates how circumstances don't dictate joy. On the face of it, his most joyful writings occurred while he was in prison! He spoke about what happened to him as a "light affliction." Paul wrote that no matter his circumstances, he was content (Philippians 4:11). Why and how could he do this? First, he looked ahead at what awaited him: Heaven, which paradoxically allowed him to find joy in the present. Contentment is the most essential element of joy. Without contentment, there is only striving.

Paul speaks about resurrection a great deal. What he says is that it gives life meaning. Without resurrection, life is meaningless—joy is impossible. Resurrection gave Paul focus and fuel. It kept him moving forward. And no matter where Paul landed, he had joy.

Jesus says to pick up your cross and follow Him. This is what Paul does. This is what you can do! This is what you must do!

To experience joy, you must not remain anchored to your past life. What happened to you must not define you. So let go of the past. The resurrection life you've been offered isn't just what you experience after you've taken your final breaths here on earth. Your resurrection life begins now! This isn't just mere optimism, believing that life can improve. Belief and faith recognize that life is more than what happened. It is what is happening now and what will continue to happen. It is what you do with your circumstances and how you find meaning in what is happening now.

Yes. A glorious life does await you. But life isn't about waiting. It's about acknowledging that your life has purpose and meaning, no matter your circumstances. How and where do you find that meaning that leads to joy? Paul states it here: "In Him, we were also chosen, destined in accord with the purpose of the One who accomplishes all things according to the intention of his will" (Eph. 1:11). You have been chosen. It is the resurrected Jesus who tells you who you are and tells you that you were made for glorious, joyful living. Jesus says, "I have told you this so that my joy may be in you and your joy may be complete" (John 15:11). God wants so much more than for you to be happy. He wants you to experience the fullness of joy! But without the cross, there is no resurrection. There is no joy.

You can continuously reset and reorient your life with prayer, bringing God into the moment, into your struggle. Recognize that you are not alone. The very same spirit that resurrected Jesus from the dead lives in you! That is the incredible gift you have been given.

Overcoming hardship and developing strength and faith creates joy. Finding purpose and meaning creates joy. Experiencing God's love and loving others creates joy. Do you want joy? Do these things. That steak or new pair of shoes or whatever may bring you happiness. But it won't last. Choose joy.

Next Steps …

- Ask yourself how much time and energy you spend on yourself trying to be happy. If it doesn't seem to work, see how giving and sacrificing for others creates a more profound sense of joy.

- Spend time in quiet contemplation focusing on the blessings in your life. Thank God. Develop greater gratitude, and offer praise for what He has given you. Remember what awaits you: resurrection!

- Choose to share laughter with friends when they are happy. Share tears when they are down. Remember, it is the sharing of your experiences that forms a connection, which will move you toward experiencing joy.

- How can you carry your cross in a way that deepens joy? If you're not sure, try to do everything you do in your ordinary life as if you were doing it for the Lord himself. See how all the ordinary becomes extraordinary.

13

FOCUS

THE APOSTLE PETER WALKED ON WATER—UNTIL HE
didn't.

I love sharing this particular Gospel story. First, because it has to do with water, and I love water stories. But more importantly, it is a vital lesson for you if you want to stay on "top of the water," metaphorically speaking, versus sink.

I've body-surfed, swum in oceans, lakes, and rivers, and skidded across the water after one of my more spectacular water-ski crashes, but I've never walked on water.

What Peter did was truly miraculous. How did he do it? In part, focus. His focus allowed him to accomplish the impossible—the miraculous. His shift in focus caused him to do what would most likely happen to you and me if we tried to walk on water: sink.

This focus should be a powerful reminder to become increasingly aware of where you place yours. Life is going on *all around you*. Yet your focus allows you to see things more thoroughly as they are, or you will see them only in part. You may not be seeing the whole picture. Therefore, you're not getting the entire story, the entire truth.Allow me to use a few examples to make this point.

If you walked into a room in my home, would you be able to describe it? You might wholeheartedly say, "Yes!"

"Completely?" I ask.

Now you sense this could be a trick question, so you hesitate. Good for you.

What if the room is pitch black? No lights. No windows. Could you still describe it? What if the room was lit well, but I put special glasses on you so that it offered only pinhole vision, and I didn't allow you to move your head around? What would your description be now?

What if you walked freely into the room but refused to open your eyes? Could you still describe it?

I want to suggest that this is precisely what you may be doing. And because this is how you choose to see yourself, others, life, or the world, you may be misinterpreting reality. You may not be seeing things completely. And because of this, you, too, may be sinking. Or angry. Or you are depressed. You may think the world is evil. That people are wonderful, or people are rotten, etc. Your focus will lend itself to interpretation and judgment.

You don't need the world, your spouse, or your neighbor to change for you to see things differently. Likewise, you may not need to change yourself to see things and people differently—you may, however, have to adjust your focus.

As a therapist, I see this frequently.

"Tell me, what's going on?" I ask the lovely young couple in front of me.

"He's a jerk. He doesn't help me with the kids and always comes home late!"

"Well, she's a cold fish. I can't ever do anything right!"

"Is this the whole picture?" I ask.

Now I ask, what do you see when you look at your spouse, your neighbor, or the homeless guy at the corner? Again, it depends on your focus and how much you see through your lens.

What if I told you that the homeless guy holding the cheap booze in one hand while holding his cardboard sign asking for help was a combat vet with a purple heart for being wounded in battle and had been decorated for heroism? Would you see him differently?

What if I asked you to see him as God asks you?

"When the Son of Man comes in his glory, and all the angels with him, he will sit upon his glorious throne, and all the nations will be assembled before him. And he will separate them one from another, as a shepherd separates the sheep from the goats. He will place the sheep on his right and the goats on his left. Then the king will say to those on his right, 'Come, you who are blessed by my Father. Inherit the kingdom prepared for you from the foundation of the world. For I was hungry and you gave me food, I was thirsty and you gave me drink, a stranger and you welcomed me, naked and you clothed me, ill and you cared for me, in prison and you visited me.' Then the righteous will answer him and say, 'Lord, when did we see you hungry and feed you, or thirsty and give you drink? When did we see you a stranger and welcome you, or naked and clothe you? When did we see you ill or in prison, and visit you?' And the king will say to them in reply, 'Amen, I say to you, whatever you did for one of these least brothers of mine, you did for me.' Then he will say to those on his left, 'Depart from me, you accursed, into the eternal fire prepared for the devil and his angels. For I was hungry and you gave me no food, I was thirsty and you gave me no drink, a stranger and you gave me no welcome, naked and you gave me no clothing, ill and in prison, and you did not care for me.' Then they will answer and say, 'Lord, when did we see you hungry or thirsty or a stranger or naked or ill or in prison, and not minister to your needs?' He will answer them, 'Amen, I say to you, what you did not do for one of these least ones, you did not do for me.' And these will go off to eternal punishment, but the righteous to eternal life" (Matt. 25:31-46).

Now, in the context, with the focus of seeing this homeless man as God wants you to see him, would you offer him a meal? Would you try to enlist some help to get him off the street? Your focus determines not only how and what you see, but it will influence your actions. And according to Scripture, your focus and how you see others have eternal consequences!

In filmmaking, the camera people spend a great deal of time ensuring they have the proper focus. The camera may be pointed in the same direction, but when they change focus, things in the foreground become crisp, whereas things in the background become blurry or vice versa. They determine what they want you to look at. On the other hand, the free life is different because *you get to choose* the focus.

What if you spent most of your day watching one news network with either liberal or conservative viewpoints? What if you're a police officer who sees crime and criminals day in and day out? What if you're a social worker who sees dysfunctional families daily? What if you live in a mansion in a beautiful, gated community? None of these things are necessarily bad, but they will shape and possibly distort your view depending on your focus. Your experience and what you choose to see will influence your actions.

As a police officer, I was trained to watch people's hands. That's what would kill you. I'd sit at a restaurant's corner table to watch the door for the potential threat to enter. It took me a long time after leaving law enforcement to change these behaviors. The behaviors changed with my change of focus. I no longer wait for the imminent attack—and mealtime has become much more enjoyable.

Depending on your focus, you, too, might be waiting for the imminent attack or for life to fall apart, even if it is unreasonable to expect it. For example, let's say you've had an unpredictable upbringing. Your mom said she'd show up to your soccer game, but she'd frequently break that promise. It doesn't matter if it was for a justified reason or not. Maybe she was an on-call surgeon, and she'd often get called in to perform life-saving surgery. All you remember is that her word wasn't good. Or your dad said he hoped you'd be able to finish going to the same high school you've attended. But because the transfer paperwork came in, he now has no choice but to move the family—the military couldn't adjust their needs to your desire to stay in that school.

Now you're an adult, and you have a new boyfriend. Things have been going pretty well for a few months, but he must cancel an upcoming date—his mom is sick. Depending on your focus, you may misjudge his actions entirely. If, in your mind's eye (conscious and unconscious memory), you see your boyfriend through the focus of your unpredictable childhood, you may jump to the conclusion that he is a flake and you can't trust him—goodbye, boyfriend. Even if his word has been good, and he's been reasonably predictable up to now.

Again, Peter walked on water—until he didn't. What changed?

Remember earlier when I wrote about the Apostle Paul and his impressive array of calamitous events? He was beaten, shipwrecked, etc. What does Paul tell you to focus on?

"… whatever is true, whatever is honorable, whatever is just, whatever is pure, whatever is lovely, whatever is gracious, if there is any excellence and if there is anything worthy of praise, think about these things" (Phil. 4:8).

Suppose Paul focused on his various calamities, the beatings, etc. I don't think he'd be the joyful evangelist we've known. Undoubtedly, his focus on the honorable and the just helped him stay on track. But Paul didn't focus on the good of this earth alone. He was able to overcome and persevere because he also kept the focus on what lay ahead.

In Corinthians, Paul says, "At present we see indistinctly, as in a mirror, but then face to face. At present I know partially; then I shall know fully, as I am fully known" (1 Cor. 13:12). Other translations say it as if we now see through a fog. In other words, our focus is just not clear—we don't see ourselves, others, or life clearly. Until we have stepped into eternity, our focus will not be able to take it all in as God wishes. But until that time, we are called to continue to shape and change our focus to see what is most important.

We aren't given the complete picture of what awaits us, but we are given clues. We are offered a glimpse, even, of God and His eternal power. Paul writes, "For what can be known about God is evident to them, because God made it evident to them. Ever since the creation of the world, his invisible attributes of eternal power and divinity have been able to be understood and perceived in what he has made" (Rom. 1:19-20). In other words, when you focus on the magnificence of God's creation, what exists here on earth, and what can be seen and understood in the cosmos, you are given a glimpse into God's majesty. Of course, this is a choice. You can focus on the bad traffic, the blemish on your face, how you've been hurt, or on all that God gives you now and what awaits.

So back to Peter … he walked on water. Until he didn't. How did his focus cause him to sink?

"Then he made the disciples get into the boat and precede him to the other side, while he dismissed the crowds. After doing so, he went up on the mountain by himself to pray. When it was evening, he was there alone. Meanwhile the boat, already a few miles offshore, was being tossed about by the waves, for the wind was against it. During the fourth watch of the night, he came toward them, walking on the sea. When the disciples saw him walking on the sea, they were terrified. 'It is a ghost,' they said and cried out in fear. At once [Jesus] spoke to them, 'Take courage, it is I; do not be afraid.' Peter said to him in reply, 'Lord, if it is you, command me to come to you on the water.' He said, 'Come.' Peter got out of the boat and began to walk on the water toward Jesus. But when he saw how [strong] the wind was he became frightened; and, beginning to sink, he cried out, 'Lord, save me!' Immediately Jesus stretched out his hand and caught him, and said to him, 'O you of little faith, why did you doubt?' After they got into the boat, the wind died down. Those who were in the boat did him homage, saying, 'Truly, you are the Son of God' (Matt. 14:22-33).

Peter walked on water until he took his eyes off Jesus and looked at the wind and the waves. Then, he sank.

You can choose. You can look at everything wrong (your storm), but most likely, you will sink. Or you can keep your eyes focused on God and do the miraculous—you can walk on the water.

Next Steps …

- How do you spend your day? What are the things to which you give your focus? Bad news? Bad people? Find several daily moments when you focus on your blessings and God's love. You may need to change your focus to the good if you find yourself worried, afraid, anxious, angry, depressed, or feeling like you're sinking.

- If particular people in your life are causing you distress, take some time and see the good that exists in them. We are all a mixed bag. The good and not-so-good live right alongside and within us. Comment to that person about the good you see in them. See how it changes you.

- If there are difficult chores and care that you must provide for others, quietly say to yourself that in serving them, you are serving the Lord himself. Remember, "Whatever you do, do from the heart, as for the Lord and not for others, knowing that you will receive from the Lord the due payment…" (Col. 3:22-24).

- Take some time each week to get out into nature. See the beauty and recognize the majesty of God's creation.

14

GRATITUDE AND
APPRECIATION

YOUR EXTERNALS DON'T HAVE TO CHANGE FOR YOU TO experience a more meaningful and joyful life, live longer, improve all your relationships, and make you a preacher of the Gospel. And this is only a partial list! You just have to embrace that one cliché, which science supports: Count your blessings.

Let me begin by making a subtle distinction between gratitude and appreciation. Gratitude asks that you take in and recognize all of the good, the blessings in your life. You realize what you *have* and give thanks. The key to becoming more grateful is recognizing the big and, more importantly, the small blessings in your life. For instance, you don't need to live in a mansion to be grateful. You can be grateful when you experience and luxuriate in the comfort of an old, warm blanket on a cold day. Having more doesn't necessarily make you more grateful. In fact, it could have just the opposite effect. If you live in a climate-controlled mansion, you are probably less grateful to possess an old warm blanket. However, if you lack the luxury of a home and adequate clothing, etc., you are more apt to feel grateful for that blanket. But neither riches nor poverty makes you grateful. *Acknowledging* and giving thanks for the blessing, big or small, is what does that.

Appreciation is somewhat more external. It recognizes the qualities of the good that exists outside of you. However, the benefits of appreciation are only fully realized when you express or comment on the good in the other to the other. You can understand the value your spouse offers your family by their sacrifice or hard work, but unless you express what you see, they may be left feeling that what they do has no value.

There are tremendous benefits to gratitude and expressing appreciation. Some research has shown that it boosts the body's immune response by lowering stress,[1] which has a positive correlation with heart health; it has been shown to contribute to an overall sense of well-being; it can ease feelings of anxiety and foster positive emotions; it contributes to the health of your current relationships while also helping to promote new ones; expressing appreciation for your partner improves relationship satisfaction and happiness; and it has been shown to increase optimism, which also has positive health benefits, including healthy aging; and as I stated earlier, it will also make you a preacher of the Gospel (I'll get to that shortly.)

Now, before I get into how you foster gratitude and appreciation, let me give you a little heads up ... the brain has a negativity bias, which means that gratitude and appreciation don't just happen automatically. I hate to say this, but your brain is somewhat wired to pay more attention to the negative, wrong, or out of place. And this isn't a bad thing—as long as it is checked!

Have you ever had an experience saying, "I just had that sixth sense that something was wrong? My gut just told me!" I hate to break the bad news, but you still only have five senses, like all regular folk. What is happening is that you are taking in little bits of information with your five senses, your brain then analyzes it, and it tells you of the threat or what is wrong. And one of the ways it does this, besides the little bell going off in your head, is that you also feel something in your gut. Remember, you sense, remember, and know with felt sensations as well as with your brain. Unless you're a Vulcan related to Spock, you know what love "feels" like. Or, if you feel rejected, you can get that sinking feeling in your gut.

This, again, is a skill that can be developed. Police officers do this when they take in little bits of information and perceive that someone might be a threat. The little pieces of information may include how

---

[1] Sansone RA, Sansone LA. Gratitude and well being: the benefits of appreciation. Psychiatry (Edgmont). 2010 Nov;7(11):18-22. PMID: 21191529; PMCID: PMC3010965.

someone holds their hands, where and how their eyes move, and the briefest of hesitations in answering a question. In this case, the negativity bias is sensing what is wrong with the tiniest clues. Of course, this isn't a skill that just police officers or other professionals use. You began developing this skill early in your life. In seconds, you could tell whether it was an excellent time to ask mom or dad if you could go out Saturday night. They didn't have to tell you they were in a bad mood; you perceived the tiny pieces of evidence.

The negativity bias warns you of a present threat and tells your brain to remember the negative. For instance, my "gut" reminds me to never, ever, ever, never again buy my wife fantastic cooking utensils for Christmas. It was a long time ago, and maybe her look and words were subtle (or not), but she'd have to go overboard and beg me before I'd ever entertain such a notion again—and that's pretty unlikely. To learn from our mistakes, we have to remember—and negativity bias helps us to do that.

But keeping this in mind, recall the chapter on Marriage. Happy couples work to remember the past fondly. Your brain will easily remember every slight and misstep thanks to the negativity bias. It takes more effort to remember the good.

Without the negativity bias, you wouldn't recognize the threat or potential harm. It allows you to see if a relationship is going south in little ways so that you can take steps to remedy it.

However, if your negativity bias is left unchecked, all you will see is what is wrong and perceive everything as a threat. It can happen quite quickly. You then may earn the nickname "Negative Nancy" or "Pessimistic Pat." But far worse, you will experience less joy, more anxiety, and fear will run your life, your relationships will suffer, and you will probably live a shorter and less healthy life.

But now that you see how and why the negativity bias serves you, you also must recognize how and why it works against you, your relationships, and your overall sense of well-being. If all you see is what is wrong, you'll be left feeling pessimistic and hopeless. There is great beauty in life and living, and if you rise above the negativity bias, you'll be more able to see and experience it.

Thanksgiving is a beautiful holiday—unless you have dish duty. But other than that, most people enjoy it. It's not just that it's socially acceptable to eat vast quantities of food and then immediately fall asleep. It's not even football. Instead, it is a day when you are asked to think about your blessings and be grateful. No presents are necessary. It's not a day about getting—just the opposite. Many people feel more compelled to volunteer on days like Thanksgiving. Gratitude does that. You give thanks, acknowledge your blessings, and feel more obliged to give to others. Recognizing how you are blessed fosters generosity.

But God doesn't want you to be grateful just some days, but *all days*. In 1 Thessalonians 5:18, Paul says that God wants you to be cheerful and give thanks no matter what is going on, no matter what happens. It's an everyday, all-the-time command. Not just when you get the new toy, go on vacation, or …

When Jesus broke bread with the disciples, he always gave thanks, even at the Last Supper, before his imminent and brutal crucifixion. You may have bad days when disasters befall you, but this is the model you've been given. Give thanks! Always!

I could easily fill up the following hundred pages of this book with examples from Scripture that have to do with giving thanks and gratitude—I won't. But there are a couple of examples that I want to highlight. In Matthew Chapter 8, Jesus met a man with leprosy. The man asked Jesus to heal him. You guessed it, Jesus healed him. Jesus *wanted* to heal him. But after the man was healed, Jesus instructed the man not to talk about what happened but to make the appropriate offering to the priest. It wasn't how the man would talk about it that would bear witness to the miracle; it was how the man would live out his life of gratitude that would speak of who Jesus was and what he had done. You are drawn to others who are grateful and joyful. And when others see this in you, they may ask about the source of your joy, just as people questioned the leper about his healing.

You may have all sorts of beliefs about how your life has fared. But there is one thing for sure. God's sacrifice offers you eternal life. What do you have to do to gain it? Accept it and believe. You don't earn or deserve it. It's a gift. And when you receive that gift and give thanks, the joy in your life becomes evident to others with your gratitude. The evidence of that gift is then how you live out that salvation life by giving and loving others. It all stems from gratitude.

However, despite being given this incredible gift, gratitude is not automatic. The best example of this, I think, is found in Luke 17. A group of ten lepers approached Jesus and asked to be healed. "Go show yourselves to the priests," He said. By faith, they obeyed. En route, they were *all* healed—amazing! But even more interesting is that only one of the ten returned to Jesus to give thanks. One.

Paradoxically, reflecting on death can also foster gratitude. Not only can you treasure the gift of this life, but the life yet to come. And when you recognize the impermanence of this life, you will be drawn to consider what matters: cultivating the relationships around you—seeing the good in others and wanting to nurture and participate in it. When you take in the magnificence of creation, you can't help but feel awe and appreciation. And, you are made in the image of God! Scripture speaks only of Man as having this trait. You are God's most splendid creation. For that, you must give thanks!

Everything in this life is fleeting. Whatever you have today may very well be gone tomorrow. But if you give thanks for what you have, whether the big or the small, you will enjoy it more deeply.

Next Steps …

• When you are grateful for those around you, you show it by demonstrating and expressing appreciation for them. And science says that expressing gratitude and appreciation mutually benefits the giver *and* the receiver—everyone benefits. Each day, take at least one opportunity to express your appreciation for another person.

- During your prayer time, spend at least a part of it giving only thanks and offering God praise. If you want a few specific places in Scripture that focus on giving thanks and gratitude, consider reading and reflecting on 1 Thessalonians 5:18; Psalm 118:24; Colossians 3:15-20; Psalm 136:1; James 1:17; and Hebrews 12:28. This is only a partial list, of course, but it will give you a start. If you can do this with your family or friends, even better!

- If you struggle with a relationship, whether it's a marriage, friendship, or family member, do an appreciation exercise. Spend several minutes going back and forth and saying, "What I appreciate about you is …" Note how much better you both feel after even a short period. Frame it with positive statements only. For example, don't say, "I like it when you don't raise your voice." Instead, say, "I like it when you speak kindly to me." Conveying appreciation helps to buffer relationships when difficulty does arise. It also increases the happiness and love in a relationship and helps to deepen it.

- Start a gratitude journal. No complaints. If this is difficult, don't worry. It may take some practice. Make sure that you focus on what you perceive as the little blessings. You may come to realize that they are not so small after all.

15

PURPOSE AND MEANING

ACCORDING TO MERRIAM-WEBSTER, "PURPOSE" MEANS: *the reason why something is done or used: the aim or intention of something.* And the definition of "meaning": *the idea that is represented by a word, phrase, etc.* (Really, "etc." is part of the definition.)

Wow. I mean, if that doesn't get you excited! After reading those definitions, doesn't your soul cry out? "Yes! I need more of that! More purpose and meaning! Especially more 'etc!'" Hardly.

The words and the definitions in themselves do not inspire. Almost empty. Purpose and meaning only charge the soul when they are filled with … What?

What do you do? Why do you do it? How do you do it? Where do you do it? To whom do you do it? You know, the big five questions. These are good questions to ask yourself as you explore purpose and meaning, or lack thereof, in your life.

There is much in life that seems mundane. Filling your car with gas, changing a diaper, paying bills, going to work, etc.—you can make out your list. It's not complicated. One of those days when someone asks you about your day, you say, "Oh, it was fine."

Think back to that "fine" day and list what you did. Is it a list of mundane? Or did you find purpose and meaning in the day? A clue as to which it was could be that you felt joy in describing what you did. If so, then it could be meaningful. Purposeful. If you look at the list and still say, "Oh, it was fine," and don't want to discuss it further, it probably lacked the qualities of purpose and meaning.

So, what must you do to have a day and a life that you could describe as having purpose and meaning? And maybe another question is, why do you want to pursue purpose and meaning?

Let me give you the answer to the first question. And it might be excellent news! You might not have to change *what* you're doing to create a life filled with purpose and meaning. You may only have to change the *why* you are doing what you're doing. I'll explain shortly.

The answer to *why* you want to pursue purpose and meaning can be as follows: life is short. Life is a tremendous gift. Like the apostle Paul says, in the end, you want to be able to say, "I ran the good race!" You don't want to take the exquisite gift of life and say, "it was fine." So, what is *your* good race?

The research says that purpose in life predicts both health and longevity—especially when confronting life's challenges.[1] Purpose helps you to reframe stressful situations so that you can deal with them more effectively. Purpose makes you tough! It gives you the strength to carry on when life seems impossible. It is purpose and meaning that makes life worth living. Let's look at an example of this.

In *Man's Search for Meaning*, Viktor Frankl wrote, "Woe to him who saw no more sense in his life, no aim, no purpose, and therefore no point in carrying on. He was soon lost."[2] In my opinion, no one in recent times has spoken more poignantly and powerfully about purpose and meaning than Frankl. No one, again, in my opinion, has the experience to speak so authoritatively on the subject. Why?

In 1942, months after getting married, Frankl and his family were sent to a concentration camp. His father died there of starvation and pneumonia. A couple of years later, Frankl and other family members were taken to Auschwitz. It was there where his mother and brother were killed in the gas chamber. His wife died later of typhus. How would you respond if this had happened to you?

---

[1] Schaefer SM, Morozink Boylan J, van Reekum CM, Lapate RC, Norris CJ, Ryff CD, Davidson RJ. Purpose in life predicts better emotional recovery from negative stimuli. PLoS One. 2013 Nov 13;8(11):e80329. doi: 10.1371/journal.pone.0080329. PMID: 24236176; PMCID: PMC3827458.

[2] Viktor Frankl, Man's Search for Meaning. From Death-camp to Existentialism: A Psychiatrist's Path to a New Therapy (ed. 1959)

After being freed from the concentration camp, he wrote extensively and became head of the neurology department of the Vienna Polyclinic Hospital. He developed logotherapy and existential analysis based on the desire to find meaning in life and the capacity to choose how to act. He dove deeply into his own experiences and those around him and used what he had learned to serve others. Purpose. Meaning.

Meaning isn't found because something happens to you. Meaning is discovered as a result of the search—it is the attempt to answer why. It's not about having all the answers but finding enough meaning in your experience until you are charged with the capacity to act, to share the lessons or insights with others for their benefit and growth. Purpose becomes determined action when meaning is understood.

Now let's go back to our questions: the "who, what, why, where, and how" as you consider how to find purpose and meaning. God says you are to live a life of purpose and meaning and discover that purpose by being a member of the Body of Christ. Paul writes, "For by the grace given to me I tell everyone among you not to think of himself more highly than one ought to think, but to think soberly, each according to the measure of faith that God has apportioned. For as in one body we have many parts, and all the parts do not have the same function, so we, though many, are one body in Christ and individually parts of one another. Since we have gifts that differ according to the grace given to us, let us exercise them...." (Romans 12:3-6). In other words, your purpose is to live and use God's gifts. You are to function as one tasked with sharing the Gospel by serving and loving others and God. Every act of service, if done as for the Lord, is purposeful and meaningful. So, what does this mean from a practical standpoint? I will start with a personal example.

My adult son is severely disabled. He needs support in feeding, dressing, showering, walking, etc. Now, as a loving father, I provide this care willingly. But if you asked me about performing these tasks, I could say I washed his hair. Mundane? Could be. But I choose to see what I do as nurturing and caring for his body and soul as though I were serving the Lord Himself.

When I do this, my efforts take on new meaning and purpose. I am cherishing and recognizing my son's tremendous value and worth. I am celebrating his life. And when I do that, I feel terrific about what I do for him as a member of the Body of Christ. These simple tasks take on meaning. What I do is infused with purpose. You could say that I am serving my son in what I do. But really, I am doing so much more. Paul reminds you, "Slaves, obey your human masters in everything, not only when being watched, as currying favor, but in simplicity of heart, fearing the Lord. Whatever you do, do from the heart, as for the Lord and not for others, knowing that you will receive from the Lord the due payment of the inheritance; be slaves of the Lord Christ" (Colossians 3:22-24). I try to make every shower a time of joy and laughter. (Luckily, my son still thinks my stale jokes are funny.)

You may not need to modify your life. You may, however, consider the *how*, *where*, and *why* you do what you do. You can go to work for a check. Or you can work with the knowledge that you are sacrificing and providing for those in your care. You can mow the neighbor's lawn. Or you can serve and love him, letting him know you care by this small act of service. You can mop the floors in a hospital and get clean floors. Or you can clean them knowing that you are contributing to the health and well-being of others who are sick. It is all about the reframing of why you do what you do. Same tasks. Different perspective.

If you do all that you do for the glory of God by offering Him your thanks and praise, and you love others in your acts of service, you are living a life of purpose and meaning. You may not be called to serve as a priest, pastor, world-famous evangelist, or great humanitarian, but you are called to love God and others with your acts of service.

You may not always know what you are supposed to do. But God says, pray—even if you don't know what to pray for. Paul reminds you that God's Spirit comes alongside you, shaping your prayers and keeping you present before the Father. That's why every act of love,

God works into good. It all becomes purposeful and meaningful. Of that, you can be assured. (See Romans 8:28).

Just as the Father was the purpose and goal of Jesus's life, He is your goal too! God has chosen you with purpose. "In him [you] were also chosen, destined in accord with the purpose of the One who accomplishes all things according to the intention of his will ..." (Ephesians 1:11).

You don't have to go anywhere to live meaningfully and purposefully. You are to live with purpose and meaning everywhere, all the time—with everything you do.

Next Steps ...

- Spend time each day reminding yourself that God has chosen you to live a life of purpose and meaning. Now make a list of what you consider your mundane chores or activities. If you are pumping gas, do you give a shout of thanks and praise for having the resources to do so? Give thanks to God for all the blessings in your life.

- Whatever your job, whether it's to care for your children, or your elderly parents, or sweep floors, try to reframe these activities as though you are serving God by serving others. Challenge yourself to do all these activities joyfully.

- God says that whatever you do for the least among you, you do unto Him. Look around you and find that person who may feel overlooked. Let them know that they matter and are loved. Perform some small act of service for them.

- If you've been badly hurt or mistreated, see if you can find meaning in what happened to you. You may even try to understand why someone hurt you. This isn't easy. But if, for example, your parents abused you, were they also abused? You may never completely understand this to your satisfaction. But as Frankl did, can you learn and grow from your experience? Can you then share your wisdom with others, helping those who have been hurt similarly? By doing this, you will break the cycle of wounding and become an agent of healing.

16

CHOOSE

WHEN I BEGAN WRITING *DEFYING GRAVITY*, MY FIRST book, I faced a parent's worst nightmare: my only two children, John and Benjamin, were diagnosed with a rare, incurable, fatal disease. With luck, the doctors said, my boys would make it into their twenties. They painted a bleak picture. Yet our lives were anything but bleak. We were bolstered by our community, who brought meals to the hospital when we couldn't leave to cook, shared tears and laughter, encouraged us when down, and reminded us through words and actions that we were loved.

My oldest, John, passed away Sept. 24, 2015. He was 24. At the time of this writing, my second, Benjamin, is still with us at 27. *Defying Gravity* speaks about how our incredible community covered us with love; how we faced each day with laughter while making way for the tears; how the awareness of death forced us to live more vibrantly, with gratitude and a focus on the here-and-now; and most importantly, how God's incredible grace would support us through it all. I share stories of miracles and some wisdom from battles fought—and, for the most part, won. This was the choice we made. And God continues to bless my family and me beyond measure.

Defying Gravity was a reflection of how my wife and I chose to live joyfully in the face of death. That choice was perhaps the most critical decision we had ever made. We provided John and Ben with the best lives we could. Of course, like all parents, we made mistakes along the way. But we did our best to share great adventures with much laughter while giving appropriate space for the tears. Every day, we had to choose how to move forward. How? We chose to play hard when it would have been easier to remain stagnant in our sorrow. My boys learned to water- and snow-ski blind; we rafted class five rapids; we laughed and wrestled; we engaged with other families and celebrated their victories; we cultivated gratitude and lived knowing that life was precious and fleeting. We couldn't keep death at bay, but we could fill each day with connection, purpose, meaning, and love. It's important to acknowledge all your feelings, including pain, loss, etc., but we chose not to let them have the last word and rule us.

I can't remember a time in my life—certainly not during my time as a professional therapist—when I've seen anxiety and depression so heightened, personal relationships so frayed, and thoughts about the future so pessimistic. But not everyone is doing poorly. Why? It begins with a choice.

Jesus chose the cross. And when He hung upon it, racked in pain, near death, He uttered, "It is finished." I wanted to say the same when I had shepherded my boys through this life and into eternity. However, life wasn't finished. Those words weren't mine to say—but how to go on?

A deeper understanding of Christ's words, "It is finished," can be better understood as "it is completed," not "it's all over." Yes, his mortal body was at an end, but his sacrifice means life is just beginning for you and me. Eternal life. Not life to death, but life to better life. And that resurrection life starts now—but you have to choose it!

There isn't a secret recipe for experiencing this revitalized, resilient, and resurrection life. But it begins with choice, and a life fashioned by God and belief.

It has become my life's passion to live a life full of joy, purpose, and meaning and to share my knowledge and experience with you. But step number one—and you may not like this—don't run from the struggle. Why? First, it has a lot to teach you. Second, it is pointless. It's not *if* trauma, death, illness, and hardship will visit you. It's when it does [visit you]. Will you be ready?

How you choose to engage in hardship will help you to rise out of the ashes and the dark into glorious life. A life of strength, joy, and holiness. This is, after all, what God wants for you. Wherever you are,

God wants to meet you there, take you by the hand, and gently pull you into an adventurous and resurrected life. But He will not force you. You have to choose to cooperate with the grace He offers.

The apostle Paul says, "Do you not know that the runners in the stadium all run in the race, but only one wins the prize? *Run to win!* Every athlete exercises discipline in every way. They do it to win a perishable crown, but we an imperishable one" (Italics mine, 1Cor. 9:24-25). That's the message. Run. Win. But running is hard.

I run. And pretty much every time I'm trudging up a mountain or doing wind-sprints, I usually think to myself, "I *hate* this! WHOSE STUPID IDEA WAS IT TO DO THIS?" Then I remembered it was mine. And more importantly, I remember it is God's command: Run! Not necessarily on my favorite mountain, but run-to-win!

Like you, there are moments when I feel I can muster only the energy to put one foot in front of the other. Not much of a run, but survival. A plodding journey. But then I am bolstered by my faith and reminded of the science behind creating a life of joy and meaning, a life so far beyond just plodding—the resilient life!

God says through the prophet Jeremiah, "For I know well the plans I have in mind for you … plans for your welfare and not for woe, to give you a future of hope. When you call me and come and pray to me, I will listen to you. When you look for me, you will find me. Yes, when you seek me with all your heart…." (Jeremiah 29:11-13). It might be tempting to believe that your welfare—which God desires for you—can be achieved easily. You pray, God answers your prayers the way you want Him to, and *voilà*! Sorry. It doesn't work like that. That isn't the Christian faith. It isn't any faith tradition I know of. God has a larger purpose!

Every great story—including yours—has at least three central characters: a hero, which is the part you want to play, the villain, who could be an actual person or maybe tragic life circumstances, and finally, the victim. That's the part you might be playing. But let's face it, who wants to be the damsel tied to the tracks?

We can all get stuck playing the victim, and maybe you've played it for so long that you've gotten comfortable in your discomfort. But I'm going to assume right now that you want more from life. A life of strength. A life of purpose. A hero's life. But remember, a hero's life is defined by the sacrifices he is willing *and choosing* to make. Before you discover that life, you must ask yourself if you're willing to make the necessary sacrifices to achieve it. Will you sacrifice your comfort to live the adventurous life God offers? Will you give up having to win the argument to win your wife back over? Will you give up your will to submit to what God wills for you? What different choices will you have to make?

Where and how do you begin this resilient journey? God's all-consuming love. Back to Jeremiah and the words God spoke about having plans for your welfare....

The prophet was speaking to the Jewish people at a time when they had been crushed and taken into Babylonian captivity. Literally and figuratively, they were stuck, separated from the life God had intended them to live. Can you identify? In their desolation, God spoke to them; He gave them the roadmap back to the Promised Land and Him. We are sometimes more receptive to hearing God, not when life is going well, but when we feel we've been taken captive by hardship, stress, and bad decisions.

In all my years as a therapist, I've never once had someone come in to see me and say, "You know, my life is pretty good. I just thought I'd pay you so ..." No. It's more like, "I'm tired of living a lie, of hurting those I say I love; I can no longer tolerate this pain; my anxiety is through the roof, and I feel like I want to die...." These are "I've-blown-it" or "I've-lost-my-way" stories, or go ahead and insert your own story. But don't lose hope. Your story is not yet complete!

Bolstered by faith, the Jewish people turned their lives around with the powerful reminder that they were loved unconditionally. They returned to the Promised Land and became a great nation again. It wasn't an overnight success story. In all probability, your story will not be either. Like you, they had to confront their fears. But as God spoke thousands of years ago, He also says to you now: "When you look for me, you will find me."

There will be times when you want to turn back. Or feel like you just can't get "there." Many great athletes, particularly those who compete in extreme endurance events like the Iron Man, don't feel they can finish. So, what do they do? They put one foot in front of another. They break down their race into feet, yards, a mile, etc., until they've accomplished the goal. As the joke goes, "How do you eat an elephant? One bite at a time." (I never saw *elephant* on any menu. And who in the world would ever want to eat one anyway? But I digress.) Maybe a more relatable saying is, "The journey of a thousand miles begins with one step." —Lao-tzu. This may be a Chinese proverb, but God speaks about your life of faith similarly. Jesus says, "And whoever gives only a cup of cold water to one of these little ones to drink because he is a disciple—amen, I say to you, he will surely not lose his reward" (Matt. 10:42). In other words, start small.

Christ invites you to pick up your cross and follow Him (Luke 9). It seems God, in His wisdom, has chosen to fashion you and me not in our ease but in the crucible of pain: The Cross. Yet, how much time do you spend trying to avoid pain—even when it is in your best interest to do the opposite? We choose not to sacrifice for our relationships. But to have thriving relationships, sacrifice is precisely what is necessary. We avoid working out and eating right. We run from suffering and struggle, yet—when we do this—our lives cannot be shaped as God intends.

There is a way to achieve a more extraordinary life. But you may be overlooking the gift that will transform your life as it now exists into that vibrant, joyful, resilient, and holy life that God offers. What is that gift?

It is the one thing that, at first glance, you probably would not recognize (understandably) as a gift. The apostle Paul certainly didn't. He speaks about it in 2 Corinthians 12.

Paul says he was given the gift of ... wait ... ready for it? *The gift of a handicap* (or, as some translations describe, *a thorn in the flesh*) to keep him in constant touch with his limitations. What? Being reminded of your limitations is a gift? Paul was initially so disturbed by this "gift" that he begged and prayed for God to remove it from his life. I know that I've done that. It seems to make sense. Isn't it reasonable to ask God to remove pain and distress from your life? But God offered Paul something much more powerful: Grace.

"My grace is enough, Paul," God said. (2 Cor. 12:9-10) And His grace *is* enough for you.

It is grace mixed with faith, and your willingness to choose the struggle, that will enable you to move from your current crises into a life shaped by God. You've got your part to play. You've taken the first step by reading this book. Congratulations! And the choices you make moving forward will bring you closer to the life your heart truly desires.

Next Steps …

- Consider the choices you're making in your life right now. It's best to start with the small day-to-day decisions. How much sleep do you get? What foods do you eat? Do you choose to exercise? Do you seek out support when you're struggling? Start making little choices to improve your health and relationships. Practice making small, good choices. This will help to prepare you when you need to make bigger ones.

- As you consider making more meaningful choices and leading a new life direction, first ask yourself what you're willing to give up. Are you ready to make choices that include sacrifice? For instance, if you want a new career, would you be ready to choose an hour of study, to prepare for that career, and give up an hour of television? What must you choose to change within yourself if you want a better relationship? Your anger? Resentment? Getting your way?

- Ask yourself if your life is where you want it to be. If not, can you track the series of choices you've made over the past weeks, months, and years that have taken you to where you are now? Try not to blame anyone else. Take responsibility for the choices, good and bad, that you've made. In this case, it may be easier to look at your big decisions first. They'll be more obvious. Then, as you consider a new direction, what are the little decisions you can make to steer your life that way? Work your way up and consider the more significant choices from there. Write this down. Don't try to choose the perfect plan. Choose a good plan. Be flexible. Adaptable. Be truthful with yourself. And most importantly, decide to take responsibility for your choices moving forward.

EPILOGUE

So you've finished reading this book. But your story is just beginning. Each moment is God's gift to start again. This is your rebirth moment.

Remember when Jesus spoke to the Pharisees and said you must be born again? (John 3) Nicodemus said, impossible. Jesus shot back, explaining that you can't enter eternal life unless you submit to the invisible, moving the visible, and become a new creation. He is speaking about salvation, but not just the life you enter when you draw your final breath. It is also about the life that begins here and now. God's Spirit moving in, and through you, you are to become a new creation.

The world is still crazy. Likely, it's even crazier than when you first started reading. But you are better prepared to deal with all the craziness because you took the time to read, reflect, and ponder some of the critical lessons that will enable you to better deal with the many challenges you face.

When I first went to the police academy, one of the many lessons I learned was how to stay alive. Pretty important. We were taught how to draw our gun smoothly and bring it up on target when using deadly force. It was *one* lesson but practiced thousands of times. The repetition, and the excellent habit formed, made it work. (Not that I ever had to use deadly force.)

Hopefully, this book has provided you with good information and inspiration. But you must practice to see the change you want in your life. You must act with intention each day. If your life resembles mine in any way, you mess up; you stumble and fall. But this is your opportunity to begin again. This isn't my message. It is God's.

So now what?

Go back to Chapter One: *Become What You Believe.* Belief will support or undermine everything you do. Jesus says, "Amen, I say to you, if you have faith the size of a mustard seed, you will say to this mountain, 'Move from here to there,' and it will move. Nothing will be impossible for you" [Matt 17:20]. You *can* move from the crazy and toward a sane, rich, and vibrant life.

Making change, escaping insanity, etc., requires not one choice but choosing to act again and again and again. For instance, you fell in love, proposed, and chose to marry. But to create and maintain a thriving marriage, you must choose to love with every thought and action. You must become more conscious of your choices, actions, and beliefs.

It's awesome to recognize that God is calling you. Pray. Listen. Reflect. Use the Next Steps as prompts. (Again, I encourage you to do this with another person or group.) My *Next Steps* are reflections to inspire action. What will be *your next steps?* It's not enough to know the information. You've got to work these principles into your life. Now go on and reread Chapter Two and so forth. Highlight, earmark, and question. Wear this book out. But most importantly, act!

If you skipped some chapters thinking, "I struggle with anxiety and control and social media addiction. So I'll go to those chapters." Please reconsider and go back and read the book in its entirety.

Why? There is a through-line throughout the book. For instance, the chapter on Focus may help you with both of these other struggles.

Your life is precious. And fleeting. This isn't a dress rehearsal. It's incredible—and somewhat frightening—to know that how you love and live has eternal consequences. But try not to worry—too much, anyway. Life is also messy. You won't do it perfectly. God doesn't ask that of you. But He does ask that you grow in holiness. Whatever you have, your relationships, and your gifts, are meant to be used and lived with eternity in mind. On that day you meet the Lord, will you know that you've done all you could with what you've been given? It's a sobering thought.

I am humbled that you've given me this time and let me into your life. Share what you've learned with others. Become that servant-leader. With God helping you, create the life He wants you to have. It is the life you want to have. You matter because you are a member of God's body. We are brothers and sisters. We are daughters and sons of Almighty God. You've got everything you need to grow; to become that new creation.

I would love to hear from you at joesikorra.com—after all, we are in this together. I wish you the very best in your journey. The whole world might be going crazy—but really, you don't have to.

Made in the USA
Middletown, DE
05 July 2023

34564064R00106